THE
MAKING OF
THE ACHIEVER

Also by Allan Cox

Confessions of a Corporate Headhunter
Work, Love and Friendship
The Cox Report on the American Corporation

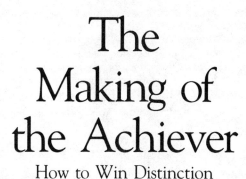

The
Making of
the Achiever

How to Win Distinction
in Your Company

by

Allan Cox

DODD, MEAD & COMPANY
New York

Acknowledgment is made to the following for permission to reproduce the material indicated:

Harper & Row, Publishers, Inc. for excerpt abridged and adapted from *Synectics* by William J. J. Gordon, copyright © 1961 by William J. J. Gordon. Random House, Inc. for excerpt from *The Conduct of the Corporation* by Wilbert E. Moore, copyright © 1962 by Wilbert E. Moore. Gene Siskel for excerpt from his interview with George Lucas. Early Morning Productions, Inc. for quote from Gordon Lightfoot's song "Race Among the Ruins," from his album *Summertime Dream.*

Small portions of this book appeared in substantially altered forms in *The Journal of Business & Society, Commerce,* and East-West Network of magazines.

Published by Dodd, Mead & Company, Inc.
79 Madison Avenue, New York, N.Y. 10016

Distributed in Canada by
McClelland and Stewart Limited, Toronto

Manufactured in the United States of America

Designed by Jeremiah B. Lighter

First Edition

Library of Congress Cataloging in Publication Data

Cox, Allan J.
  The making of the achiever.

  Bibliography: p.
  Includes index.
  1. Executive ability.   I. Title.
HD38.2.C69   1985   658.4'09   84-13729
ISBN O-396-08471-0

Learning is finding out what you already know. Doing is demonstrating that you know it. Teaching is reminding others that they know as well as you.

RICHARD BACH in *Illusions*

Leadership is a virtue rather more widely subscribed to than understood.

The legitimate occasions for leadership in corporations largely involve change. Only routine management, not leadership, is needed in stable and secure organizations. The leader then sets new goals and justifies them, sets performance standards, and encourages followers to new effort. He is an innovator, moralizer, demonstrator, teacher. And as such, he is a dangerous man.

Leadership of the type and quality that corporation executives sometimes like to attribute to themselves as "great leaders of men" is usually, and fortunately, the product of a mistaken ego. Real crisis situations may provide opportunities for truly individual leadership. If the crises are manufactured, the strategy is likely to wear thin. And in the ordinary course of events such individual qualities must be severely restrained for the sake of organized and orderly action.

WILBERT E. MOORE
The Conduct of the Corporation

What they (business executives) seem to forget is that strong leadership is anathema to a democracy. The whole idea is that our democratic system itself creates a strong, viable society, and that has been our history. We don't need strong leaders, and we have not attracted strong leaders except in times of crisis.

JOHN NAISBITT
Megatrends

Contents

III

JUDICIOUS

IV

RESOURCEFUL

Introduction:
The Achiever's Profile

We have entered a particularly gratifying, spirited period in American business. I believe we have turned a corner. After taking our lumps in both the domestic and foreign press for poor products, rewarding the short view and neglecting the customer, American corporations and their executives have begun to come off the defensive and rightly feel good about themselves again.

I further believe that we deserved much of this criticism, and are beginning to feel better about ourselves because we realize we *weren't* paying attention to the proper matters and now want to set things right. Our priorities *were* out of whack, and while we told ourselves we were making the most of our capital investments, this harvesting attitude led us away from long-term commitments that served the best interests of our customers. Taking care of our customers takes care of our companies—over the long pull, and that's what counts. We had forgotten that, but again are beginning to remember.

The "back to basics" mentality that is prevalent today is a reflection that performance and substance take precedence over rhetoric and image. American business is indeed reasserting itself in response to aggressive foreign competition and the self-deception that had crept into its management practices and policies. This is overdue and welcome. Moreover, I have no doubt we are on the road back to commitment and mastery.

However, in the midst of this renewed flexing of American business muscle, we are likely to hear a growing chorus from corporations and the press about the need for more "leadership" and for more executives who are "true leaders" and not "mere managers." *Charisma* is likely to be dredged up again and put before us as a model. "Give us strong leaders," we'll say. "Show us a man or woman with charisma," we'll demand.

I would like to suggest that it is not "leadership" we need during this wonderful new start-up, but *achievement*. Leadership is a term that has become such a catchall that it is largely meaningless, or at best, has a definition known only to the speaker or writer who uses the word.

As an indication of this, it is instructive to note that the Random House College Dictionary offers twenty-nine definitions for the verb *lead*! By meaning so much, it ends up meaning little. Further, the primary definitions convey no overriding sense of distinction: (1) "to take or conduct on the way; go before or with to show the way"; (2) "to conduct by holding and guiding"; (3) "to influence or induce; cause"; (4) "to guide in direction, course, action, opinion, etc."

Carrying this analysis a bit further, *leader* has ten definitions in all including: "a person or thing that leads"; "a guiding or directing head, as of an army, political group, etc." *Leadership* itself is defined as: "the position or function of a leader"; "the ability to lead"; "an act or instance of leading"; "the leaders of a group."

All of these definitions bring us to the point of realizing that in most usages "leader" refers to someone who holds a *position* or has attained a *title*, whether formal or informal in nature. We then are left with the necessity for an adjective to describe the *quality* of the leader. Consequently, we speak of progressive leaders, aggressive leaders, and those who are bright, articulate, balanced, energetic, perceptive, and so on. But there are also leaders to whom we apply such labels as petty, corrupt, slow, fearful, mediocre, short-sighted, self-serving, unimaginative, and so on. Clearly, there are extraordinary leaders, poor leaders, and average ones. To repeat, it is the modifier—not the noun—that gives us the picture.

What does it *mean* when a candidate for political office

claims to bring "new leadership" to the tasks at hand? Or when an organization boasts that it has shown "leadership?" Or when we say of our corporations or governments that we need "leadership?" Usually, "leadership" translates to whatever actions we prefer, such preference—like beauty—being in the eye of the beholder. In reality, for organizations or individuals to convince us they have shown leadership, *they have to be able to point to their achievements*. Then and only then do we begin to see something we can get a grip on.

Distinction intrudes our thought, however, when we consider the same dictionary's definition of achievement: "something accomplished, as by superior ability, special effort, or great valor." Often when we speak of *achievers*, we use modifiers, but they aren't actually necessary. With apologies to Gertrude Stein, an achiever is an achiever is an achiever. We may say that a child is an underachiever, but what we mean by this term is that he or she *could be* an achiever, but *isn't* one as yet. "Achiever," unlike "leader," is not a title. It is a category of accomplishment among persons.

To be sure, there are degrees of achievement. Some people are better at particular things than their associates are. For example, some members of a championship track team may be able to outperform other members in the same event, even though the minimum standards for making the team are exceptionally high to begin with. Moreover, we all know we may be achievers in some endeavors while not in others. So to reemphasize, it is our *performance* in an area—not our position or title—that determines whether or not we are achievers. Ironically, while a leader may turn out *not* to be an achiever, it is the achiever who *leads* and inspires with his or her accomplishments. He or she is someone to emulate!

Therefore, our present emphasis rightly should be on achievement because that is what squares with our renewed insistence on performance—in a hard, but good-sounding word: *commitment*.

The achiever, then, is a person who sets goals and meets

them. He or she is someone we can count on to get the right things done in a superior way and *keep* getting them done. In other words, the achiever never stops learning, growing, striving. Finally, today's achiever—working in a highly collaborative setting—is someone who gets things done through others.

By directing our attention to achievement rather than "leadership," we eliminate a great deal of fuzzy-headed thinking and increase our personal accountability.

Concerning *charisma*, it is not my intention to denigrate it, but simply to point out that it is horribly overrated. My experience is that charismatic persons tend to be short-termers. Unless they are company founders, they often don't stay in one place for very long. Wanting to check out my impressions, I went back to the writings of Max Weber, the German sociologist who, in the early part of this century, gave us the concept of charismatic authority. Weber confirmed my thoughts with these words:

> "The only basis of legitimacy for it (charismatic authority) is personal charisma, so long as it is proved; that is, as long as it receives recognition and is able to satisfy the followers or disciples. But this lasts only so long as the belief in its charismatic inspiration remains."

We are notoriously fickle followers. What happens to our enterprises when we desert our charismatic leaders?

Rapid change and crisis are what call for extraordinary leadership and charisma. And in no way would I deny that these conditions are present in certain American corporations. But our current "back to basics" disposition is a reminder that for most of us, the more things change, the more they stay the same. Undeniably, what we have to cope with still is getting the job done in a caring, distinctive way. What we face is not a persistent call to Herculean tasks, but faithfully living up to our everyday commitments. That's where we are. As mundane as this may sound, this is achievement, and it's what makes the world go round. Despite what you may read or hear from quick-fix snake oil salesmen about how to "make it" in the executive suite, it is this kind of steady competence that will bring you the highest psychic and monetary rewards in your work over time.

I would not want my vocabulary to be without the word "leader." Indeed, I use the word throughout this little volume. But what I mean by it is no more than someone who is "in charge" of some function or project, and who is called upon to exercise authority and influence upon others. My use of it is not meant to conjure up images the likes of Napoleon Bonaparte, Winston Churchill, or Franklin Roosevelt.

The Making of the Achiever is concerned with measuring, describing, and improving the performance of the actual hero who is needed now more than ever in the service of the American corporation. That hero is the *achiever*, and while he well may be charismatic, he more often is not; while she is undaunted, she does not necessarily call dramatic attention to herself. Rather, he or she gets the job done in a caring, distinctive way.

Being a consultant specializing in executive search and executive development for twenty years has put me in a unique position to observe executive achievement—or lack of it— across a total array of corporate functions, in a wide variety of industries, in companies that succeed, coast and fail at what they aim to accomplish. Not only has this work resulted in my interviewing and evaluating thousands of executives for specific high-level jobs, but it required that I spend hundreds of hours sitting across the desks from chief executives and other senior officers who shared with me their ideas about the management of their companies.

My hope is that these pages provide a fresh look at old truths. What few new trails I blaze have only to do with fashioning a scheme to understand the dynamics of executive achievement and providing the means for making them work for you. In short, my goal is simplicity, and to produce a persuasive argument showing that executive achievers are marked by four main qualities. These achievers are: (I) other-centered, (II) courageous, (III) judicious, and (IV) resourceful.

Naturally, you might wonder how I chose these four qualities. True enough, I well might have chosen three, or six, or any number. However, from among all the qualities characteristic of achievers, these four, according to my lights, best sum up what these rare persons are all about. In other words, to my mind, *they constitute the profile of the achiever.*

The book is organized into four main sections and two appendixes. Each section examines one of these four broad qualities of the achiever. Appendix A (for those whose interests run in this direction) charts a slightly different course to deal with the impact of bureaucracy on the achiever, and how corporations can work to minimize its destructive elements on all their people. Appendix B contains answers to short quizzes that begin each chapter.

The four sections of *The Making of the Achiever* are further divided into five short chapters each, making twenty in all. Each chapter contains my observations on one critical thought-and-action pattern characteristic of the broad quality being examined in the section of which it is a part. Moreover, every chapter gets your attention right from the start by opening with a quiz that measures and rates your performance and adherence to that pattern. Your numerical score and rating are likewise determined for each of the four sections as a whole. Finally, a grand total score, arrived at by adding up those of the four sections, constitutes your *achiever index.*

An additional important feature of the book is that each chapter concludes with an exercise titled "Written Action Plan," designed by you, that shows you how to improve executive performance in specific ways and raise your achiever index.

As should begin to be clear, this book's aim is to put or keep you on the road to *hard mastery of essential soft subjects.* Accordingly, it deals solely with developing your competence in critical areas that are intangible. For unless you attain such mastery, you cannot become an achiever. Therefore, you will find no pat formulas here. Distinctive, lasting success in the executive suite cannot be bought so cheaply. If you think it can, reading this book will waste your time. But if you agree that hard mastery of essential soft subjects is what buys the genuine article, *The Making of the Achiever* will reward you. Its quizzes, observations, and exercises will let you know *by score* exactly how far along you are in these subjects, and how you can assure yourself of improved performance, increased commitment, and continued progress in your career.

How to Use This Book

While every chapter is only one piece of the larger picture of which it is a part, it is meant to be a freestanding subject in itself. That is, if it were to be read alone, it should offer its own worthwhile lesson apart from any other. While my intention in writing this book is to provide you with a comprehensive and in-depth treatment of the requirements for achievement, I'm assuming that you, like I, are more accomplished in some areas than others. Consequently, it is likely some chapters in this book will be of more immediate interest and help to you than others.

Be that as it may, each chapter is structured in exactly the same way. Each has three parts. Each begins with a short quiz to force you quickly to take stock of yourself in its subject (for example, making judicious decisions) before I address that subject in an essay that follows. The purpose of the quiz is not to "outsmart" you or be tricky in any way. As you will see, it is easy to discern what the "right" answers are to the questions. However, since no one but you knows what your answers will be, you have every reason to be completely honest with yourself in your responses. You will tally your answers for each quiz and derive a score that will give you an indication of your level of competence in the subject under discussion in the chapter. For our purposes here, scores and ratings in the "fair" or "poor" categories constitute *non-achievement*.

The essay of each chapter comprises its second part and requires little comment. It is simply my observations on what it means to be competent in the subject under consideration.

The third and final part of each chapter is the written

action plan. This demands the most effort on your part. After you have taken the quiz and computed your score, and then read the essay, you are called on in the third part to complete three exercises which make up *your* written action plan. These exercises require rigorous thought and immediate commitment from you. They constitute the "how to" part of this book to ensure that it is more than a mere intellectual experience. It is the part that aims at changing *your* thought-and-action patterns to improve your performance and raise your *achiever index.*

Let me caution you on the exercises, however, and follow up on a hint I dropped earlier. I believe it would be a mistake for you to approach the exercises of every chapter with equal fervor. I say this because, as will be made clear, they ask a great deal of you. If you were to try to do all of them in short order, unless you are a certified genius, and a triple-A time manager, you wouldn't have any time left for your job itself!

By all means, take every quiz, read each essay, and peruse all the exercises to learn which ones may have something special to offer you. On the other hand, on those quizzes where your scores indicate you need to grow in an area, embark on the exercises of *that* chapter energetically. Another alternative would be to take all quizzes and read all essays before doing any exercises. In short, do whatever suits you best, but be sure to save all your written action plans so you can refer to them in the future. There will be value in that, and you will be able to note your progress. What is important to remember about the exercises, no matter how you elect to do them, is that while demanding, they also are *enjoyable* and *revealing* of self and others. Moreover, they are *rewarding.* Doing them will put you into firm contact with many of your neglected inner resources.

I believe this is a book for now and a book for later. To repeat, some of its subjects will be of more use to you now;

others of more use to you at another time. Keep it around. It can become a long-time (if threadbare) companion. Let some time go by, reread a particular essay, then retake a quiz or two. If you have put the exercises into practice, I'm confident that you'll be pleased with your growth in the interim.

THE
MAKING OF
THE ACHIEVER

I

OTHER-CENTERED

The self is as the sound of one hand clapping.

ZEN PROVERB

WE LIVE in the midst of the rhetoric of *revolutionary change*. With the publication of Alvin Toffler's *Future Shock* fifteen years ago, we were made aware of how the future comes rushing in on us. Accordingly, more than ever, corporations purport to be disciples of strategic or long-range planning so as not to be caught addressing today's problems with yesterday's solutions.

A good part of the rhetoric of revolutionary change is directed to our being executives in a new age of information. Data is being made available to decision makers and all knowledge workers at breakneck speed in gargantuan quantities. Yet as political scientist Andrew Hacker has pointed out, who hasn't always had to deal with information in the performance of his or her tasks? Moreover, just how fast has this "information age" hurtled itself upon us? Not very. The electronic computer has been with us for well over a generation, and we are just now getting around to seeing that it won't hurt us. This explains the long delayed growth in the personal computer business.

Twelve years ago, one of the nation's major commercial banks retained me to conduct a search for a director for the electronic funds-transfer segment of its operations. Six weeks later, the bank's top management abandoned the search because they concluded their consumers would resist having their funds moved in and out of their accounts without "feeling" their money. Even today, banks experience much more difficulty than they expected in getting their customers to use their "efficient" automatic tellers.

I'm not saying we all don't suffer dislocations as the currents of society shift direction or emphasis. But for the bulk of our lives and work, we deal with evolution, not revolution. To my mind, the rhetoric of revolutionary change is overblown, and we typically are called upon to perform not at battle stations, but in situations most accurately described as routine. As a matter of fact, many of us wish change would occur more quickly.

A simple example will help make my point. Whenever the question comes up among observers and participants in business as to which large American companies are the best managed, a few names invariably surface. Such companies are Procter & Gamble, IBM, GE, Caterpillar, 3M, Hewlett-Packard, and Standard Oil of Indiana. Several other fine firms could be cited, but these should suffice.

While all these strong corporations are known for quality products and good management of their people, what is most notable about them is that they have earned and sustained their top reputations over many decades. Some have done so for over a century.

In order to survive—and thrive—for so long a time, they obviously have had to deal effectively with change. Permanence is proof of adaptability. They are not dinosaurs. Yet anyone who knows these companies at all realizes that one quality they all share in common is orderliness. They are not a swashbuckling bunch.

Evolutionary change, rather than the sweeping change of the popular consciousness, is the concern of these standard-setting corporations. Proven over time, this concern has shown itself to be well placed. In contrast, many of the darlings of the "high-tech revolution"—where coping with "unprecedented change" is a daily operating requirement—have begun to go under, only proving that they didn't understand change at all, and have been caught up in an artificial world. They lost sight of the fact that high-tech is not an end in itself, and that its job is to serve "low-tech." The P&Gs, GEs, 3Ms and IBMs are acutely aware of this.

Moreover, large numbers of the thriving participants in our burgeoning entrepreneurial "class"—while not denying the contribution and opportunity residing in "high-tech"—do not hear these two words as a siren song. On the contrary, an examination of this group—which constitutes an ever-growing share of our economy—shows that almost three-fourths of them are engaged in operations and services that are decidedly "low-tech."

The abundance of information available to executives today actually can be a nemesis, and offers no guarantee that the *quality* of decisions will be improved. On the contrary, many executives "escape into information" and avoid the difficult, emotional aspects of decisions—such as the proper timing of them—that make them more likely to be the right ones.

So the achiever's main concern is not to be overly taken with the ramifications of revolutionary change, but to foster rich, enduring, effective relationships with his work associates. Therefore, it is appropriate to focus initial attention in this book on the importance of being *other-centered* rather than self-centered in the quest to get the right things done in the right way at the right time.

Five thought-and-action patterns go into the making of the other-centered executive: (1) warmth; (2) the willingness and ability to listen; (3) an encouraging nature; (4) the disposition to think positively; and (5) the eagerness to share self, time, and information with others.

To begin your *achiever development program*, simply turn to the first chapter and conduct an assessment of your *warmth*.

1

Warmth:
Unsung Trait of the Corporate Hero

To test your *warmth*, please answer the following questions by marking the response item that most clearly matches your typical behavior. Remember, you have everything to gain by being objective in your replies. No one but you will see the results.

As you will notice, the purpose of the quiz is not to make the questions difficult to answer, but for you to take an inventory of your actions and measure your performance.

1. Do you smile when greeting your subordinates?
Usually/Often _____ Sometimes/Seldom _____

2. Do you shake hands with a firm grip?
Usually/Often _____ Sometimes/Seldom _____

3. Are you unwilling to poke fun at yourself among associates when you make a mistake?
Usually/Often _____ Sometimes/Seldom _____

4. Do visitors and subordinates feel uncomfortable in your office?
Usually/Often _____ Sometimes/Seldom _____

5. Are openings in the department/function you manage sought after aggressively by many?
Usually/Often _____ Sometimes/Seldom _____

6. Do you praise/thank your subordinates for their daily accomplishments?
Usually/Often _____ Sometimes/Seldom _____

7. Are your subordinates hesitant to initiate activities and projects

without your instigation?
Usually/Often _____   Sometimes/Seldom _____

8. Do you *enjoy* going to lunch with your subordinates?
   Usually/Often _____   Sometimes/Seldom _____

9. Does a sense of team play and pride prevail in the department/
   function you direct?
   Usually/Often _____   Sometimes/Seldom _____

10. Do you "save up" criticisms of your subordinates' perfor-
    mance until a formal review session?
    Usually/Often _____   Sometimes/Seldom _____

MY WARMTH INDEX

To determine your score on the *warmth* quiz, check your answers
against the correct ones listed in Appendix B.

For each correct answer, give yourself one-half point. Add
up the correct answers and mark the rating category that corresponds to your score.

My score _____   _____ Superior   4.5–5.0
(Warmth Index)   _____ Good   4.0
                           _____ Satisfactory   3.5
                           _____ Fair   3.0
                           _____ Poor   0.0–2.5

BEING WARM

Including *warmth* as an essential characteristic of the achiever is at first likely to bring a snort from the hardheaded. Yet numerous images in our everyday language show how anyone who hopes to move among people with the intention of having influence on them must demonstrate this specific quality.

A warm room is considered inviting. A warm spring day portends a sense of renewal. A warm smile encourages affiliation while a cold stare creates distance. A warm reception generates appreciation while a chilly one breeds resentment. A warm handshake displays vigor; a cold one, lack of it. A sunny disposition is desirable; a glacial one is not.

It amazes me that some of the most simple truths of the ages—such as the need for warmth in directing the activities of others—are ignored by large numbers of executives who take themselves too seriously while not taking their associates seriously enough. Warmth is not only the province of the do-gooders and naive, but also of those top executives who thrive in their jobs, have longevity and a string of promotions with their companies, and over the long pull can point to the most significant operating results.

Warmth Attracts

In my experience as an executive recruiter, no outcome has proved to be as predictable as this: those corporate clients who have great warmth always attract the most capable executives to their ranks.

Here's how this happens. I define warmth as *the appetite for showing and being shown acceptance*. This two-way process, begun by the client, puts the prospective recruit at ease and presents the client and job candidate to each other in the most authentic way possible. That is, client and candidate alike keep the playing of contrived roles to a minimum. Each gets to respond to the other on the basis of who-he-truly-is rather than the fruitless who-he-wants-the-other-to-think-he-is.

All of us are aware of articles and books written to help candidates eager for jobs sell themselves to interviewing corporations. In addition, companies grow ever more sophisticated in techniques designed to win them executives whose services they seek, along with the cream of the graduates of prestigious business schools.

Ordinarily these candidate guidelines and corporate activities do not have much impact because they can be seen through easily and count for little unless they are coupled with potential working relationships based on warmth. In other words, they are pointless unless they are in support of relationships spawned in an interview situation between a prospective superior and subordinate where warmth is a critical ingredient. When executives talk about the element of *chemistry* that is necessary to working well together, I take that to mean that warmth must be shared between one executive and another.

The executive who projects warmth attracts not only the best management talent from the outside, but quality performers *within* the organization flock to that executive as well. In fact, the latter is even more the case because such a key executive's management style has been more exposed and tested, and his record of performance placed under longer, more penetrating scrutiny.

The appetite for showing and being shown acceptance is a bridge-builder between people. Whether we admit it in ourselves or not, it is part of human nature to want acceptance. We enjoy it to the hilt when it comes our way. The difference between the mediocre executive and the distinctive one is that one waits for the bridges to be built by someone else, while the other builds them himself.

Warmth Spurs Initiative

By building bridges between people, warmth spurs initiative. The top executive who shows and is shown acceptance is an achiever who stimulates voluntary actions and programs by subordinates. The warmth they enjoy in their relationships with him or her constitutes an invitation to attempt their best, test their imagination, stretch their resources, and function autonomously. It affords them the opportunity to take risks because they sense his or her optimism about them; the belief that they will succeed more often than they fail. Out of these experiences, they grow enormously as executives and are far more productive to their companies.

What I'm describing is not some sort of trendy, manipulative management style that may have grown out of the sensitivity training and encounter group movements, but a simple, straightforward, honest means of supervision in the workplace founded on mutual respect.

Actually, many of the warmest, most effective top executives I've known and worked with are blunt, gruff, authoritarian curmudgeons! Despite their crusty exteriors, there is often a twinkle in their eye and a wry smile that accompany their criticisms or demands. And the accomplishments they insist on from their subordinates are the most convincing proof of all of the faith they have in those subordinates.

Robert Six, the man who built Continental Airlines, was just such a curmudgeon during his long tenure. Few more demanding chief executives have existed. Hard-driving, sometimes volatile, often exasperating to his subordinates, he nonetheless was loved by many and respected by all who worked at the airline. A perfectionist who fashioned Continental's peerless standards of service, he could be extremely critical of his peoples' performance. Yet throughout his company and the airline industry as a whole, he was known as a man of abundant personal warmth. Though he could be harsh, he also had a winning smile and was the first to praise and reward superior performance by his lean, efficient staff.

In 1972, on the occasion of being named "Man of the Year" by UCLA's Executive Program Association, this is what Robert Six had to say:

> It has been my observation that a desperate management in a frantic effort to implement employee communication frequently treats its people like spoiled brats. . . .
>
> May I suggest that there are many millions of workers who actually, honest-to-God, like their jobs and are proud of their skills? Accepted doctrine seems to insist that employees hate work, hate the boss and have to be coddled and cajoled into punching a clock because they would much rather be down at the library improving their minds or out on the beach playing in the sand.
>
> Ladies and gentlemen, despite what you hear, most people enjoy going to work in the morning. Honest! They find their tasks interesting—even challenging; their fellow workers likeminded people with whom they can share occupational concerns. Many grow to be their best friends. The cadence of the job has a healthy rhythm. Their rewards are tangible and satisfying.

These words, spoken early in the last decade, reflected the views by which Six had practiced management effectively for over thirty years. He set store by them right up to the day of his retirement as chief executive in 1980.

Warmth Pervades

Warmth is catching. It is easy to discern those companies where warmth in management has caught on. From first contact with the headquarters receptionist to the head of custodial services in an outlying plant, a visitor who walks the halls of a warm company and chats with its people, senses the team-play and pride that pervade its atmosphere.

Also apparent in this setting is an easy, affable lightness—a corporate sense of humor among executives. While there's no question about their caring deeply about their business, they aren't overbearing in their mission. In addition, crispness prevails over sloppiness. Practicality prevails over high-sounding nonsense. Commitment to mastery prevails over mediocrity. Substance prevails over rhetoric. Performance prevails over credentials and admiration for the CEO prevails over cynicism.

In the cold company, opposite conditions exist. Grilling prevails over collaboration. "What have you done for me lately?" prevails over long, consistent service. Subterfuge prevails over direct action. Dressing down prevails over praise. Pessimism prevails over expectation. Fear prevails over boldness. Politicking prevails over cooperation. *No* prevails over *Yes*. Avoiding the CEO prevails over seeking his counsel.

I ended the litany of the warm and cold company characteristics by referring to the CEO in each case. I did so because he is the central figure in his company's makeup. More than any other individual, he sets the tone. Since he is responsible for ultimate results, he generally is given the freedom by his board of directors to govern the company as he sees fit. With such responsibility, it follows that he should have the authority to manage according to his lights.

How a company goes, then, depends on those lights. If, for example, he has reached his pinnacle of career success in a cold company, he is likely to reinforce a management style that rewarded him by getting him where he is. After all, he was selected for his key post because he *conformed* to the standards deemed desirable by the board of the company. The same is true of the CEO who resourcefully threaded his way upward through the warm company. He, too, will gravitate toward directing his company according to guidelines and methods that brought him success.

The warm company will take care of itself. Therefore, my concern is for the cold one. Its glacial mentality courts failure through self-defeating impulses and habits. Its sole long-term hope rests in a CEO who achieved success by moving on one course but is aware that continued success can be achieved only by charting another.

There are more chief executives in these straits than we realize. The inertia and resistance they face from the organization accustomed to the cold way of doing business are staggering. Such CEOs need to inspire their right-minded subordinates by making clear to them that success is dependent wholly on their helping him carry out this crucial shift in managerial style and company spirit.

The achiever stands ready to give such help and return the warmth.

WRITTEN ACTION PLAN

Suggestions for changing your thought and action to raise your *warmth* index.

1. List the names of five successful executives with whom you work and consider warm. Write out at least three ways for each that warmth contributes to their success. For example, under one you might write, "Sam makes clear to his subordinates that he expects them to try new things. Even when they screw up, he's there with a pat on the back and a smile. He gets burned sometimes, but over the long haul, he makes it pay."

For Carl, you might write, "His firm handshake and unpretentious manner let you know immediately you're OK until you prove otherwise. Even when he fires someone, he never destroys that person's sense of dignity. People will do anything to work for him."

For Susan, you might write, "She gives enormous energy over to getting to know her people really well. It's obvious she cares about their off-the-job concerns, too. Even her bosses confide in her."

2. After itemizing these fifteen-or-more bridge-builders, write the names of two associates with whom you work, but by whom you do not feel accepted. Work at overcoming their

resistance by adopting some of the patterns of the five executives in your "admired" group. Write down which patterns seem most appropriate for you to adopt with each of
the two associates. Take action on them starting tomorrow.

3. Write down the names of two associates with whom you
work and to whom *you* do not show acceptance. Build bridges
to them by adopting patterns from the above group. Write
down those that seem most appropriate for each associate
and take action on them starting tomorrow.

In time, if not right away, you'll find these changes come
more naturally to you than you expect, and it will become
increasingly easy for you to make a habit of them in dealing
with most people. While you won't win everybody over, you'll
see a positive impact in the lion's share of all with whom
you have contact.

2

Good Listening:
The Vital Link in Management
Communication

To test your *listening*, please answer the following questions by marking the response item that most closely matches your typical behavior.

1. When talking with an associate, do you finish his/her sentences?
Usually/Often _____   Sometimes/Seldom _____

2. Do you apologize to a subordinate who complains to you about something you have done before he/she has fully "said his/her piece"?
Usually/Often _____   Sometimes/Seldom _____

3. Do you look beyond the literal content of a speaker's comments to you? To their timing, location, and manner?
Usually/Often _____   Sometimes/Seldom _____

4. Are you an animated listener? Do you nod to encourage the speaker? Do your facial expressions show interest? Do you admit it when you're having trouble being interested?
Usually/Often _____   Sometimes/Seldom _____

5. Are you a "debater" type listener? Do you make your conversing partner *prove* his/her points?
Usually/Often _____   Sometimes/Seldom _____

6. Do you keep listening and speaking in fairly equal parts in discussion with another?
Usually/Often _____   Sometimes/Seldom _____

7. Do you risk speaking your opinions to your conversing partner even though you don't know that partner's thoughts on the matter under discussion?
Usually/Often _____   Sometimes/Seldom _____

8. Do you give thought to converting your questions to statements in order to clarify your position?
Usually/Often _____   Sometimes/Seldom _____

9. Do you make yourself accessible for discussion to subordinates and peers?
Usually/Often _____   Sometimes/Seldom _____

10. Are you hesitant to admit you don't understand something that your discussion partner is saying?
Usually/Often _____   Sometimes/Seldom _____

MY LISTENING INDEX

To determine your score on the *listening* quiz, check your answers against the correct ones listed in Appendix B.

For each correct answer, give yourself one-half point. Add up the correct answers and mark the rating category that corresponds to your score.

My score _____   _____ Superior   4.5–5.0
(Listening Index)   _____ Good   4.0
                            _____ Satisfactory 3.5
                            _____ Fair   3.0
                            _____ Poor   0.0–2.5

PRACTICING LISTENING

No act in all of management—save that of thinking itself—is given as much time as the spoken word. Yet no other act in all of management is as grossly underutilized as the one in which one executive speaks to another.

The reason for this is simple: we are notoriously poor listeners. Students of communication estimate that we listen with about 25 percent efficiency. And this is when the conditions for listening are good. When the environment for listening is less than adequate, or when ill feelings exist between speaker and listener, our efficiency is much less.

Of course, there is a difference between hearing and listening. There is also a difference between examining listening in a literal sense—what is factually spoken and comprehended at a given time—and examining the listening *process*—all the factors, including what's left *unsaid*, surrounding the oral communications link between executives.

Becoming adept in this process—a kind of listening with a third ear—brings immediate rewards to the achiever. Let's take a look at it.

What We Do Too Soon

In a word: *respond*. When an associate embarks upon a subject he cares about, gets two or three sentences into his argument or presentation, and then is met by your counter that begins with "You know what I think . . ." he's just been had. Premature response is not only one of the bad manners of dialogue, it blocks the passage of useful information.

We typically offend the speaking party and negate his contribution in three ways: (1) explaining, (2) reassuring, and (3) apologizing. While these activities seem innocent, and are desirable and necessary in the proper time and place, they have harmful effects on the listening process when we employ them prematurely.

In explaining, our intent may be to help the speaker-now-turned-listener understand a complexity he has over-looked, but the result may mean missing an insight he has gained. In reassuring, our intent may be to encourage him in a difficult task, but the result may mean missing an imaginative new approach he has conceived. In apologizing, our intent may be to admit the error of our ways, but the result may mean shutting out a beneficial critique. In all such cases, whatever their particular blend, our impatience guarantees a spoiled opportunity.

What We Shouldn't Do at All

There are innumerable fruitless, self-defeating pursuits in which all of us as executives engage. This is not because we have a death wish in any managerial sense, but because we tend not to be perceptive about our real motivations in deal-ing with others. We need to understand the hidden purposes of our chosen behavior among people with whom we con-verse.

The late Karen Horney, a psychoanalyst who achieved prominence in the earlier half of this century, aptly noted that in all our relations with people we either move toward, away from, or against them. If one observes the listening process and uses this simple three-part analysis, it becomes apparent that behavior we shouldn't engage in falls into these latter two categories, namely, moving against or away from people.

As a listener, by *moving against* a person, I have a couple of options. The first is to fall back on my status and supe-riority; the second is to intellectualize the content of the speaker's words. The purpose of both types of behavior is not to learn, but to maintain some sort of control over my speak-ing associate.

In falling back on my superiority, I can be condescend-ing and make the speaker feel stupid for having come to me with his ideas. Or I can engage in interpretation, and bless him with the bounty of my omniscience as to why what things are happening, when, and where. Or worse, I can just out and out scold him for being so negligent, shallow, uncommitted, tardy, or whatever.

In intellectualizing the content of my speaker's words, I overlook the "how" of speech. By concentrating on the literal message, I deny her emotion and the *manner* in which she brings me this message in this place at this time. I may also play "lawyer" and make her prove her contentions. Or I may "get even" by pointing out how her current point of view or actions are at odds with her past. Finally, I may make a joke about her reasoning to show her that I'm not taking her idea seriously.

Moving away from people is shown in passive listening. Here, the listener's behavior says to the speaker that his or her concerns just aren't important enough to gain the listener's attention, or that they are threatening in some way. Bored, deadpanned expressions are characteristic of the listener who is in retreat. So is playing stupid. And, most importantly, so is passing the buck.

What We Should Do More Often

I begin the consideration of what we should do more often with the notion that if a person speaks fully and freely, he seizes a measure of his potential. If this is so, as I believe it is, it makes all the sense in the world for the would-be listener to encourage such speaking. The quality of listening improves in these exchanges because the quality of speaking improves. In addition, valid information is given and received, and performance on the part of speaker and listener improves.

In wanting to encourage full and free expression, we come face to face with Karen Horney's remaining alternative: we have to move *toward* people. For example, if I want to be a competent listener, and am not going to rely on a good exchange with my partner just happening by chance, I have to take action. I have to move toward him or her by being honest, vulnerable, and direct myself. In other words, to be a good listener, I also have to be a good speaker and be ready to take the initiative in speaking fully and freely to encourage the same from my discussion partner.

Incidentally, this point doesn't contradict my earlier one about premature response. There, my concern was for taking initiative unwittingly designed to ward off another's strong thoughts or feelings. Here, it is for taking the initiative in such a way as to *welcome* those same thoughts or feelings.

Too many executives come to a discussion as *getters* with little willingness to give as well. Such people can never be good listeners because it doesn't take long for others to realize their game and, consequently, feed them partial or tainted information.

By being honest, vulnerable, and direct with another, one practices the other side of listening, the vital other half of the listening process. In so doing, he doesn't deny his own thoughts and feelings on a subject or project, but spells them out—taking the risk that his partner may reject them or think them foolish. Day in and day out, good listeners know that risk pays off.

There is one major way we can take that risk and move toward others effectively. Ironically, it requires only a simple change in an exceedingly common but misdirected approach to discussion. That is, *we should convert our questions to statements*. Think about it. The late Frederick Perls, founder of Gestalt therapy, made this pithy observation: "The question mark is the hook at the end of a statement."

Just think how often we ask a question, not to gain real information, but to make a point. Think how often we ask an incriminating question to put someone on the spot. Think how often we're self-conscious about an idea, so we throw up a trial balloon and say something like, "George, I see that Apex is getting serious about roller bearings. What do you think about that?" What George is being asked to do is play a guessing game rather than give a straight answer based on his expertise.

How much better it would be to get to the heart of the

matter and improve the listening process by handling the issue this way: "George, Apex is getting serious about roller bearings. I'm counting on you for your thoughts on this, but I think we can beat them to the market and beat them bloodier yet after they arrive. There are risks, I know, but I am for taking the plunge. Tell me what you think." George now can speak forthrightly, and his comments will be taken seriously, even if he disagrees, or offers a counterproposal or modification. He'll contribute in the future, too.

To be sure, I'm not saying asking questions is always wrong. Often, there are times when we need to invite the participation of others in discussion by asking questions, and when we need to elicit factual information or coveted opinions. But I am saying we will improve the quality of our listening by determining on what occasions, for example, we ask "Why should we do that?" when we really mean "I don't think it makes sense to do that."

Concluding, it needs to be said that we improve our listening by moving toward others in another way: by giving them our time—in the proper amount and frequency. The major vehicle for all functions of management is the listening process. By giving time, the achiever is saving time.

WRITTEN ACTION PLAN

Suggestions for changing your thought and action to raise your *listening* index.

1. Think of one executive with whom you have an oral communications problem. That is, the listening process somehow is hindered between the two of you. Joint participation is lacking. Write down that person's name, and after it, indicate whether you are moving *away from* or *against* him or her. If you are moving away, jot down your typical actions that hinder the listening process. For example, among other things, you might write, "With Marge, I always expect her to begin the discussion."

Do the same if you are moving against. In this case, you might include something like, "No matter what my intentions, I always seem to enjoy making Jim look a little stupid."

Repeat this exercise with two other associates.

2. List the names of five associates with whom you enjoy good mutual listening. These are people you *move toward*. Record your typical actions that enhance the mutual exchange and absorption of valuable information with each of the five.

Now write how you can put these actions into practice with the three associates with whom you have listening difficulties. Begin implementing these practices immediately, and repeat this assessment process in the future whenever you experience listening difficulties with others.

3. Write out ten questions you asked of associates today (or yesterday if you're attending to this in the morning). Ponder which ones were not asked truly to gain information, but rather to make a statement. Put a check mark next to those questions and convert them in writing to statements.

Learning to spot the use of questions as judgments or subterfuge—and eliminating it—will aid you in the entire oral communication process with your co-workers.

3

How to Encourage Our Associates and Ourselves, Too

ENCOURAGEMENT QUIZ

To test your *encouragement*, please answer the following questions by marking the response item that most closely matches your typical behavior.

1. Do you *seek* to work for bosses who push you, stretch you?
   Usually/Often _____ Sometimes/Seldom _____

2. Do you *avoid* working for bosses who would push you, stretch you?
   Usually/Often _____ Sometimes/Seldom _____

3. Do you believe yourself capable of adding a worthwhile dimension to an associate's life?
   Usually/Often _____ Sometimes/Seldom _____

4. Do you avoid intervening in an associate's life?
   Usually/Often _____ Sometimes/Seldom _____

5. Do you enjoy helping make an associate courageous?
   Usually/Often _____ Sometimes/Seldom _____

6. Do you show enthusiasm over the long pull for an associate's display of courage through your voice, facial expressions, and gestures?
   Usually/Often _____ Sometimes/Seldom _____

7. Do you avoid imposing on your subordinates your ideas of *how* a job should be done?
   Usually/Often _____ Sometimes/Seldom _____

8. Do you encourage your boss?
Usually/Often _____   Sometimes/Seldom _____

9. Do you depend on others for encouragement in your work?
Usually/Often _____   Sometimes/Seldom _____

10. Are you determined to reclaim some neglected strength?
Usually/Often _____   Sometimes/Seldom _____

MY ENCOURAGEMENT INDEX

To determine your score on the *encouragement* quiz, check your answers against the correct ones listed in Appendix B.

For each correct answer, give yourself one-half point. Add up the correct answers and mark the rating category that corresponds to your score.

My score _____   _____ Superior   4.5–5.0
(Encouragement Index)   _____ Good   4.0
                            _____ Satisfactory 3.5
                            _____ Fair   3.0
                            _____ Poor   0.0–2.5

PRACTICING ENCOURAGEMENT

It strikes me that encouragement has become ever a larger part of our management vocabulary while diminishing its share in our inventory of action. In short, word has replaced deed. Our increasing use of the verb *to encourage* betrays our thinking of it as mild support—a bland dish indeed—when compared to what it really means: *to make courageous!* Achievers focus their attention on the latter.

Encouragement-as-vocabulary giving ground to encouragement-as-vigorous-deed does not require a dashing demeanor. Rather, it means to make courageous in daily involvements whether they be critical or seemingly mundane. Melville, in describing Starbuck, the chief mate on the ill-fated ship in *Moby Dick*, hits the bull's-eye: "Starbuck was no crusader after perils; in him courage was not a sentiment; but a thing simply useful to him, and always at hand upon all mortally practical occasions."

No one can deny that to make courageous—whether it be ourselves or others—when facing all "mortally practical occasions," is a quality useful in exercising our duties as executives. I would like to explore the subject of encouragement briefly with the intent that its vigor be reclaimed to serve all achievers.

Being Encouraged

The most telling set of examples that illustrates our inclination *to be* encouraged is seen in our reaction to charismatic people. Franklin Roosevelt stiffened us by proclaiming, "We have nothing to fear but fear itself." John Kennedy, making us wonder if we had been irresponsible, said, "Ask not what your country can do for you, but what you can do for your country." Martin Luther King, Jr. heartened a dispirited people with his, "I have a dream."

Our warm response to the inspiring words of such leaders shows the power and importance of crowd behavior in their being able to build or reflect a large consensus. We feel emboldened and ennobled while members of such audiences. But what is important to remember is that until those feelings are converted to personal action entailing risk, we remain simply *inclined* to encouragement rather than being courageous.

A less amorphous way of being encouraged is commonplace in corporate life. It usually occurs when a subordinate finds himself reporting to a superior who has the capability to stretch him. This kind of one-to-one interaction frightens us, but that rare individual willing to risk mistakes and embarrassment at the hands of a boss who will not accept less than his best in a set of circumstances is allowing himself to be made courageous. Willingness to seek out such relationships, or not run from them when they are presented, are acts of courage in themselves.

Encouraging Others

An executive indicates he or she possesses high self-esteem when he or she encourages an associate. But being presumptuous enough to share in the responsibility of making another person courageous is not to be taken lightly. It, too, has its risks. Was General Patton wrong in slapping his battle-fatigued soldier, hoping to stir him from cowardice? I certainly don't know, but he was presumptuous enough to do it and it cost him a much-desired command.

Perhaps the pistol-toting general can be faulted for macho behavior, but to one degree or another, his sense of presumption is precisely what is called for if we are to encourage another. It means we consider ourselves capable of adding a worthwhile dimension to another person's life—even, occasionally, when he doesn't welcome it. The trick, a tough one to be sure, is to intervene without imposing.

Imposing in a person's life is coercive and constricting. Its purpose is self-serving to the imposer. It says, no matter how subtly, "do it my way." On the other hand, intervening is open-ended. It maintains the presumption by believing it needs to be there, but as a guide, not a dictator. Its purpose is not coercion, but development. It says, "Do that thing you're afraid of; do it now; I don't care how you do it, but do it well, as I know you can!"

One receives a tremendous payoff from intervening in another's development of courage. The payoff is exhilaration. This squares with the wisdom of the ages that man is a social animal. Consequently, such a reward for altruism, occurring just as often in the competitive climate of commerce as anywhere else, is as it should be.

The exhilaration derived from intervening successfully in another person's development of courage is the tip-off that emotion itself has a large part to play in the encourager's entire role. No encourager will succeed in his task if he is unwilling to demonstrate his emotional stake in the process. He must not be hesitant to show his enthusiasm in voice, facial expressions, and gestures over the long pull. He must be strong in sharing his own values insofar as they serve as examples for having his charge be firm about his. Put another way, in his own particular style, the encourager must be willing to inspire, and eschew the current sophistication that labels such caring as hokey.

One last item should be mentioned in helping make others courageous. The encouragement process moves in four directions, not just downward. Subordinates are not the only executives who benefit from being encouraged; so do peers (sideward); and so do bosses (upward). The fourth direction (inward) is what I deal with next.

Encouraging Ourselves
Whether being encouraged, encouraging others or ourselves, our nemesis in the process is *risk*. While both business risk and emotional risk may be intertwined when an executive acts courageously, it will be more fruitful in this context to confine our thoughts to emotional risk.

The beauty in encouraging ourselves is that risk falls

right into our laps. We alone have the initiative for action, for making ourselves courageous. Alfred Adler, the great psychologist and physician, defined courage as overcoming a hesitating attitude, of obliterating the "yes, but" view of life. That means to me that I must act on those strengths of mine that have atrophied because of *disuse!*

Each of us has unique strengths that for some dim purpose we have kept hidden—even from our own view. It is bringing these out from the closet and acting on them that takes courage. That's the risk. The fact that we've disowned these strengths proves that for some reason they scare us.

Because of our selection of certain dubious career goals, we sometimes condition ourselves to think we have certain strengths that we don't, to want certain strengths that we shouldn't, and to cultivate certain strengths that are inappropriate for us. With all that gyrating, we overlook our real strengths.

In short, a disowned strength is a *value*, something you care about down to your bones, but shy away from because if you acted on it, you think you would be looked on as silly, inappropriate, inept, or downright weird. Further, since it has been in disuse, putting it back to work in your life will render you embarrassingly awkward for awhile, or longer. Right?

Wrong! A disowned strength put to work is imagination. It's resourcefulness. It's energy. It's insight. What's most important, it is distinctively you, what you have going that nobody else does. A corporation needs what you have to offer. You simply have to find a way to give it. Succeed and you'll discover that your disowned strength sets up a positive chain of events that feeds on itself. People will notice and appreciate your contribution. They'll see your verve. Motivation issues dissolve because a disowned strength is natural to you. It provides its own fire power. You have taken back a piece of yourself you had discarded and now you're stronger for it.

Recently, I gladly accepted an invitation to speak to a

conference of general managers of the most profitable, large food company in the United States. The theme of the conference, beamed to each participant, was: YOU ARE THE DIFFERENCE.

They really have something there. Innovation doesn't come from big budgets. It comes from courage.

WRITTEN ACTION PLAN

Suggestions for changing your thought and action to raise your *encouragement* index.

1. List the names of the last five to ten bosses you have had. Put a check mark beside each one you thought stretched you, who consistently accepted nothing less than your best performance. If you have only one or two check marks, it is likely you have been passive in seeking growth supervision opportunities.

If you have been passive, or have not been sought after by the "get-the-right-things-done" superiors in your experience, you need to take more control of your work and career. List five superiors in your company you believe would have much to teach you and *to whom* (if you shed your timidity) you would have much to contribute. Start winning more attention on your current job by "making yourself courageous" and acting on what you believe in. Then you won't get caught thinking "I could have done that" when you see someone else get credit for what you wanted to do, but were afraid to try.

Make a point of getting to know those five bosses. Let them know what you're engaged in. Don't brownnose or badger; just let them see what you're excited about, what you've accomplished, and how those accomplishments help the functions they now manage.

2. List the names of all the people you supervise directly. After each name, write either "impose" or "intervene." With whomever you intervene, keep it up. With whomever you impose, stop it and start intervening. Intervening is the ideal way you can help make your subordinates courageous and exult in their jobs. If you're inclined to write "ignore" beside a name, you are abdicating your management responsibility.

3. Take a separate sheet of paper, turn it on its side, write the word "STRENGTHS" at the top, and divide it into four columns. Title the first column "strengths I think I have but really don't." Title the second, "strengths I want but shouldn't." Title the third, "strengths I cultivate but shouldn't." Title the fourth, "strengths I have, but have disowned."

Obviously, this is an exercise in self-assessment and it requires all the objectivity you can muster. The key is to admit to yourself the ways in which you engage in self-*image* actualization rather than true self-actualization or fulfillment. Therefore, column four is the most important one. This is the list you should compile that tells you what you believe in, but for the press of career concerns and wrong turns may have lost touch with. This is where your values are. And it is within these values that your courage may lie dormant.

Review this sheet monthly, add to it whenever appropriate, and heed!

4

Thinking Positively: What It Is, What It Isn't

To test your *positive thinking,* please answer the following questions by marking the response item that most closely matches your typical behavior.

1. Do you reject the notion that thinking positively is an attitude that you can cultivate in yourself?
   Usually/Often _____ Sometimes/Seldom _____

2. Do you find yourself engaged in hopeless causes?
   Usually/Often _____ Sometimes/Seldom _____

3. Are you good at selecting involvements where you have a distinctive contribution to make?
   Usually/Often _____ Sometimes/Seldom _____

4. Do you relate your work activities to some higher purpose, to seeing how it improves the lot of mankind?
   Usually/Often _____ Sometimes/Seldom _____

5. Do you dread having your opinions known by your opponents?
   Usually/Often _____ Sometimes/Seldom _____

6. Do you engage your associates' strengths rather than focusing on their limitations?
   Usually/Often _____ Sometimes/Seldom _____

7. Do you avoid acknowledging discouragement when it comes?
   Usually/Often _____ Sometimes/Seldom _____

8. Do you set unrealistic goals for yourself?
Usually/Often _____ Sometimes/Seldom _____

9. Do you focus your attention on completing your tasks to the exclusion of enjoying *performing* them?
Usually/Often _____ Sometimes/Seldom _____

10. Do you celebrate your accomplishments?
Usually/Often _____ Sometimes/Seldom _____

MY POSITIVE THINKING INDEX

To determine your score on the *positive thinking* quiz, check your answers against the correct ones listed in Appendix B.

For each correct answer, give yourself one-half point. Add up the correct answers and mark the rating category that corresponds to your score.

My score _____
(Positive Thinking Index)

_____	Superior	4.5–5.0
_____	Good	4.0
_____	Satisfactory	3.5
_____	Fair	3.0
_____	Poor	0.0–2.5

THINKING POSITIVELY

I have noticed in my contacts with achievers in education, health, religion, charitable volunteer organizations, and business, that no one with whom they deal is given short shrift as much as the negative thinker.

Is this so because such leaders engage in wishful thinking and cannot tolerate matters as they really are? Hardly. These people are responsible for results, and though being designated a leader in our rhetoric carries a degree of glamour, there is no disputing that leadership activity (whatever that is precisely) must be carried on in an atmosphere known pejoratively as *bureaucracy*. Bureaucracy does not deserve its bad press because it is no more or less than the organization of people and tasks on a large scale. But it is complex, to be sure, and no achiever can make his way through bureaucracy's web by being simpleminded. No, there are other reasons why the negative thinker is given the fast shuffle in favor of the positive thinker, who is known to bring an extra dimension to the enterprise.

What follows are remarks on positive thinking: (1) what it isn't, (2) what it is, and (3) how to cultivate it.

What It Isn't
Few scenes are sadder than the one in which a person is struggling with an impossible set of circumstances, trying desperately to believe he or she somehow will conquer all. And nothing is more infuriating than to watch and hear some shallow superior point to the person's failures in such circumstances and say, "You're just not thinking positively; you can do it," then quickly move on because he also finds the circumstances unbearable and can't see a way out.

The reason so many of us are repulsed by the term *positive thinking* is that it often gets dredged up for tawdry causes in places where false inspiration is used to manipulate or control others. Unfortunately, this powerful and legitimate tool of inspiration is misused by individuals intent on serving their own ends rather than those to whom the inspiration is directed.

The lesson from political life is clear: rash promises and the call to new hope among dispirited people lead to even greater depression and apathy when those promises go unfulfilled and those hopes are proved unjustified. Thinking positively is not manipulating or being manipulated. It is not being grandiose. It is not being naive. It is not being falsely enthusiastic or optimistic. Perhaps most important, it is not denying periodic, normal outcroppings of discouragement.

What It Is

I also might have said that thinking positively is not a legislated experience. That is, you can't practice it merely because someone tells you to. Nor can you extend it to one area of your life, the home, for example, but exclude it from work or the community. This brings us squarely to what positive thinking is, namely, *the lifestyle-wide mental capacity to seek and find workable, beneficial options*. Life constantly presents us with obstacles and opportunities. Positive thinking is the means for dealing constructively with them.

The lifestyle-wide capacity I mention boils down to an attitude—an affirmative attitude about the nature of people, things, places, and circumstances. Since it is an attitude, this capacity can be cultivated. They who thrive and they who are thought to be creative, lucky, or leading charmed lives are people who have cultivated this attitude to the point of a high art.

How to Cultivate It

Executives who get results always have options. Executives who have options always get results. Ironically, the whole management development discipline typically rests on the notion that a company will get better results by making better managers of its people. This is the wrong philosophy. A company needs to think in terms of making better people of its managers. That's human development instead of management development, and it can be started best by educating executives on their inherent capacity to develop options and perform admirably via the full employment of their *affirmative emotions*. The slogan Delta Airlines has used for many years—"Delta is ready when you are"—is an example of this.

Let me cite another example, this time a mind-bending one, from the world of medicine. It is described in Norman Cousins' book, *Anatomy of an Illness*. It is Cousins' own moving story of how he defeated a critical illness by rejecting a hopeless set of options—in this case the usual medical ones—for those which he created out of the employment of his own positive inner resources.

While traveling abroad, Cousins contracted a ravaging virus which led to a collagen disease. Within a few days after returning to the United States, he was in a New York City hospital with the connective tissue in his spine so inflamed and disintegrating so rapidly that he could barely move—and then only with excruciating pain. The prognosis was grim: irreversible and crippling. One of the legion of specialists caring for him pegged his chances for recovery at one in five hundred.

After days of exhaustive tests, a growing disenchantment with hospital routines which he thought were harmful to the curative process, and a treatment program based on a virtually hopeless prognosis, he called in his doctor to announce an audacious treatment program he had devised himself.

He would move out of the hospital and into a hotel room. He would stop taking heavy doses of aspirin, which had been prescribed to reduce the inflammation of his connective tissue (but produced bad side effects), and replace it with doses of ascorbic acid. On his own, he learned that ascorbate, or

Vitamin C, had been shown to be effective in some cases in combating arthritis and other collagen diseases, but in such large doses might induce severe kidney damage. Given the circumstances, Cousins thought the risks were worth taking. His doctor swallowed hard, but approved the program.

The last part of his treatment program is beautifully startling. Cousins reasoned that since it was well known to medicine that depressive moods and panic act as multipliers of disease, why not embark on a regimen for the encouragement of positive moods to enhance healing?

Accordingly, he enlisted the help of his friend Allen Funt. He had Funt send over all his old films of "Candid Camera" for him to view. Over a period of several days, he steadily gathered strength, gained additional hours of needed sleep because of a marked reduction of pain, and literally laughed his way back to health.

This was the beginning of a recovery process in 1964 that became total. Today, Cousins enjoys golf, tennis, horseback riding, and other pleasures such as a full turning radius of his head—absolutely unthinkable when he first came down with his dread disease. His "miracle" against such odds is so well respected in the medical fraternity that, though a layman, he now serves on the faculty of UCLA's School of Medicine and is consulting editor of *Man & Medicine*, published by the College of Physicians and Surgeons, Columbia University. Cousins concludes that what got him started on the road to recovery more than anything else was a full and systematic expression of his affirmative emotions!

As I've said, thinking positively is not a legislated experience. It can be cultivated only by the person who has seen the light—who senses the need for it in his own life. It is at this point, then, that such a person begins to realize that the resources for seeking and finding workable, beneficial options lie *within*. Cultivation becomes mainly a matter of recognizing personal resources and acting on them. After all, what is creativity for most human beings other than resourcefulness in mixing existing elements? As Alfred North Whitehead reminded us, everything since Plato is a footnote.

If you are eager to act on your own resources, I offer the following recommendations:

- Choose your involvements carefully. Hopeless causes waste effort and thought that are spent better elsewhere. Select those circumstances where you have a distinctive contribution to make.

- Be honest with yourself about current prospects as they truly exist.

- Relate your activity to some higher purpose. See how in some way (no matter how small) it improves the lot of mankind. If it doesn't, do something that does.

- Believe in yourself enough to take a chance. Learn to speak your mind and take a stand. This builds self-confidence. You'll be identified to your opponents, but also to your supporters.

- Engage the unique strengths of your associates rather than focusing on their limitations. Concentrate on what's right about a situation rather than what's wrong.

- Acknowledge discouragement when it comes. Admitting temporary defeat allows you to step back and gain fresh perspective.

- Eliminate grandiosity. Don't be afraid to admit a mistake. Don't make impossible demands of yourself or set unrealistic goals. Winning half a loaf is an exhilarating experience when no bread at all was thought likely.

- Savor the race as well as its finish.

- Celebrate your accomplishments.

Taking action on these items sets off a self-reinforcing, interwoven cycle. They are all both causes and effects of the affirmative emotions.

WRITTEN ACTION PLAN

Suggestions for changing your thought and action to raise your *positive thinking* index.

1. Describe in writing the circumstances leading up to two situations in which you are a central figure, and about which you feel discouraged. In both, include two or three mistakes you made that contributed to the current state of affairs. For example, you might write, "I had a good idea here, but I had to showboat and try to sell it 'upstairs' myself. If I had gotten Ben to help me with it, it probably would have sailed through because he's got such credibility with those folks. Instead, I choked and blew it."

Second, in each case, briefly describe what you did *right* along the way. Don't make excuses, but simply acknowledge the redeeming features of your actions, even though the results were not what you hoped.

Next, in your best judgment, list three or four options you have for each situation, including *doing nothing*—simply letting it go. Select which one is best *at this time*.

Do it! Whichever option you choose will be the right one.

2. Take a separate sheet of paper for each person who works directly under your supervision. Write one name at the top of each sheet. Take your time, and below each person's name list only his or her strengths (no limitations permitted!). Include every strength that comes to mind. None lacks significance.

Place a check mark beside each strength that the subordinate is expressing well on the job. For every strength lacking a check mark, identify one way in which you will encourage that subordinate to express that strength.

3. Survey your entire life over the past year and start jotting down what you have accomplished. Include any item in which you take a measure of pride. Let your mind roam far and wide. Your list can range from cleaning out the garage, to swimming a mile, to spending more time with the kids, to being awarded a patent, to winning a coveted promotion. Whatever.

After you've finished, lean back and celebrate how resourceful you've been. Don't be afraid to crow a bit about these accomplishments to your spouse or a close friend. You won't be bragging; you'll be showing and reinforcing what you value, and that you welcome hearing about his or her "milestones" as well.

5

Today's Management Imperative: Sharing Self, Time, and Information

SHARING QUIZ

To test your *sharing*, please answer the following questions by marking the response item that most closely matches your typical behavior.

1. Do you believe executives in a corporation cooperate with each other more than they compete?
   Usually/Often _____ Sometimes/Seldom _____

2. Do you *disagree* that the corporation is an appropriate place for the practice of altruism?
   Usually/Often _____ Sometimes/Seldom _____

3. Are you committed to being a person "who makes the times" in your own sphere at work?
   Usually/Often _____ Sometimes/Seldom _____

4. Do you treat every piece of paper in your in-box as being of equal importance?
   Usually/Often _____ Sometimes/Seldom _____

5. Do you neglect to set aside large blocks of time to do creative work and planning?
   Usually/Often _____ Sometimes/Seldom _____

6. Have you been criticized by associates and subordinates for isolating yourself from them?
   Usually/Often _____ Sometimes/Seldom _____

7. Do you resent having to attend group meetings called by your boss?
   Usually/Often _____ Sometimes/Seldom _____

8. Do you resent having to call group meetings that your subordinates attend?
   Usually/Often _____ Sometimes/Seldom _____

9. Do you withhold information useful to your associates that will be of competitive advantage to you in your career?
   Usually/Often _____ Sometimes/Seldom _____

10. Do you make sure your voice is heard on subjects where you have strong (and you believe knowledgeable) opinions?
    Usually/Often _____ Sometimes/Seldom _____

MY SHARING INDEX

To determine your score on the *sharing* quiz, check your answers against the correct ones listed in Appendix B.

For each correct answer, give yourself one-half point. Add up the correct answers and mark the rating category that corresponds to your score.

My score _____   _____ Superior   4.5–5.0
(Sharing Index)   _____ Good   4.0
                          _____ Satisfactory 3.5
                          _____ Fair   3.0
                          _____ Poor   0.0–2.5

SHARING SELF, TIME, AND INFORMATION

Among the pioneers of modern psychology, it was Alfred Adler who focused on *aggression* as the moving force of human behavior. His conviction on this matter led him in 1911 to break from the Vienna Psychoanalytic Society, of which he was president, and repudiate its view—propounded and vigorously defended by Freud—that sex was the supreme human drive.

Later on, functioning freely outside the severe theoretical strictures of the Vienna Society, Adler began to move away from an emphasis on biological views of behavior. Such emphasis had been implicit in his belief in an aggressive drive—a force within man that pushes him. Instead, he began to stress the social nature of mankind and the *purpose* that is served by human beings *choosing* to behave as they do. In short, he shifted man from being an object of fate to an agent of choice. Rather than being biologically driven, human beings are future-oriented, choosing behavior in accordance with a purpose. It was he, therefore, who first called attention in a formal way to man as a goal-seeking being!

Adler believed we all are born feeling that we are in a minus position. The inadequacies, dependency, and length of human infancy virtually guarantee it. In attempting to overcome this "minus" position, early on we set up an irrational goal of striving for superiority. Superiority over things; superiority over people. This behavior can be seen in every child (and in all adults, at times). Because this goal is irrational, it is unattainable, and leaves us with a feeling of inferiority. Hence, Adler is the father of the superiority and inferiority complexes.

As Adler's thoughts on striving for superiority supplanted his emphasis on an aggressive drive, so his concept of *social interest* began to emerge as an initiative we possess to counter our irrational striving for superiority. By social interest, Adler meant the natural, altruistic interest we have in our fellow man; the interest we have in a better world and in helping, supportive relationships; the interest we have in pulling and working together for a common cause, of collaborating, of sharing our resources with each other.

Adler's views are an appropriate psychological backdrop for business achievers. He left us with a framework for understanding (1) how it is natural and proper for us to seek mastery; (2) how we have the freedom of choice as individuals to seek that mastery rationally or irrationally; (3) how our goals can be harmful or helpful; and (4) how the exercise of social interest ensures that our goals are enhancing rather than destructive for self and others.

Adler stated that each of us comes into this world in possession of social interest, but it is underdeveloped. It needs to be cultivated if a person is going to reach his or her full human stature. Since managing is a human and interpersonal enterprise, it follows that this is an arena ready-made for the practice of social interest. Accordingly, I hope to show how *sharing*—rather than competition-run-amok—is characteristic of executives who are achievers and most admired on the job.

Sharing Self

In managing, in a practical sense, the sharing of ourselves is paying homage to the division of labor. It is also a sort of human version of the interchangeability of parts. In this case, the "parts" are not identical, but they each have their place, and if "engineered" properly, contribute to optimal functioning of the "machine."

To share ourselves means giving to our co-workers nothing less than what is *distinctively us*. We all have basic abilities, training, education, and exposures that make us more or less a match to our job descriptions. But what is distinctively us are those qualities that make up an added dimension and cause pleasant head-turning among our associates.

We all have been through the experience of having a

fellow executive show us impressive skills or resources we didn't know he or she could call upon until normal routines were interrupted and an altered set of action or thinking was called for. Such resourcefulness is always pleasing to behold, but more importantly, we realize it is on such occasions that our organizations are extremely well served.

Dramatic needs make apparent the necessity for bold action and outstanding leadership. World War II England cried for a Churchill and got him. Corporations in dire straits must call upon a swift, confident turnaround artist or face demise. These kinds of illustrations lead us to the conclusion that "the times make the man."

On the other hand, most of us go through our careers working for companies that, even if not wholly imaginative or progressive, turn in good journeyman performances day after day. While bold action is not so patently in need in these situations, who would not agree that they provide an enterprising executive with an opportunity to move his company off dead center in his or her own small way? These are circumstances when the woman or man can "make the times."

The play-it-safe corporation needs the person who makes the times. The executive who remembers that his real job is to share with the organization what is distinctively *him* is acting boldly, and by making such a contribution is proving he is just such a person.

Sharing Time
All of us are too familiar with the cliché about time being our most valuable resource. I can think of no single topic that has been dissected, analyzed, preached about, and re-monstrated over more than the use or misuse of time. Surely no subject has been more of a boon to business seminar leaders than that of time-management. I have led a few such seminars myself. Sifting out from the tonnage of paper and years of lecturing that have been devoted to time management, I know from personal experience of three rules that

work. One: set aside large blocks of time to do creative thinking, planning, or writing—such as manuals, reports, and the like. Let nothing (nothing!) violate these times. Two: don't treat every piece of paper in your in-box as if it were equal to all others. Three: do first things first, second things hardly ever!

Executives I marvel at the most, and who strike me as the most effective, are bright and appear to be a little lazy. They are effective because they are uncompromising about setting and sticking to priorities. They are masters at following the three rules above. This leaves them more free to (1) cope with the unexpected crisis or opportunity, and (2) share more time with their associates.

Since a corporation is a social organization, it is a requirement that executives be accessible to each other. Managers who insulate themselves from their peers and subordinates under the gruff guise "that they have work to do," are making a workstyle decision that is personally stultifying and harmful to the enterprise. These executives—even at the most senior levels—who work, work, work, are usually astonished to learn that where their efforts and careers are concerned, things don't go according to plan.

There's no argument that some companies make a fetish of committee meetings. The quip that "if Moses had been a committee, the Jews would still be in Egypt," has real merit. But committees don't have to be a waste of time. If they are run flexibly and informally enough, they can be a fruitful way of sharing time.

Studies have shown that both the quantity and quality of communication drop in proportion to the physical or geographical distance between parties. This is true even in so simple a matter as when people who have had adjacent offices find themselves moved to separate wings on the same floor of an office building. This becomes progressively more the case as they find themselves separated by floors, different buildings, cities, and dispersed geographical regions.

If the quantity and quality of communication are so fragile even in simple spatial changes, it becomes clear how hard good executives work at making sure they cultivate community spirit and the "we feeling" among their peers and subordinates. They do this by repeatedly going out of their way to share time with them.

Sharing Information

Information can consist of observations from our experience, opinions right or wrong, beliefs, philosophies, specialized knowledge from our education and training that we exercise on the job, and facts as we see them. It also includes articulating what we don't know.

As achieving executives, we are obliged to share information we possess with our associates up, down, and across our corporations. As with self and time, withholding information that is useful to the organization is competition-run-amok. Moreover, such self-serving actually runs counter to the development of self-esteem.

In no way am I denying that we often have to work with an executive who is so closed to ideas and knowledge from others that we are left with no alternative but to let him hang himself. But aside from that, we need to guard against our silence due to timidity, or delaying our gospel with messianic anticipation, awaiting the time when we can appear with the words of salvation in a cloud of glory.

For those companies clearheaded about decision making, information is power and the means of achieving corporate mastery. Many executives erroneously believe that the purpose of sharing information is to enable the working group or committee to reach *consensus* on an issue and course of action. They believe that this is democratic management in practice. On the contrary, the idea behind democracy is the selection of various leaders to whom we collectively entrust authority and decision making. True democratic management welcomes information. *Everyone has a voice and the chance to participate.* The point of democratic management is not to reach consensus, which usually translates to mediocrity, but to choose from among all options presented and discussed that *one* which, in a given case, is likely to lead to outstanding results.

Speak up!

WRITTEN ACTION PLAN

Suggestions for changing your thought and action to raise your *sharing* index.

1. Write out three main ways you mismanage time. For example, you might write, "I travel too much to see people I enjoy seeing, but don't need my supervision, and avoid seeing people I don't enjoy, but do need it." Or, "I agree to chair meetings before the individuals involved have prepared themselves for what will be discussed. That way, I not only waste my time, but theirs as well."

List three major projects you're concerned with presently where this poor use of time compromises your management performance. Pledge to eliminate these practices. Today.

Over this coming weekend, take time out to contemplate three new enabling time-management practices to replace these debilitating ones. Write them down, and review them at the end of each day over the following two weeks to see that you're adhering to them.

2. Don't eat lunch alone at your desk. First of all, everyone—including you—needs a break to avoid going stale. Go to lunch with someone you work with who will benefit from sharing time with you. Make sure you "spread the wealth" and avoid playing favorites, however. Lunch doesn't have to be a big deal or consume a lot of time. It well may involve a workout with someone, followed up with a yogurt and fruit juice. Or, on occasion, it may require a more elaborate affair to celebrate some group accomplishment. Whatever, don't miss this valuable opportunity to give a piece of yourself and a piece of your time. Your luncheon partner is not the only one who will gain from the association!

3. Name two important projects where your superiors hold you accountable—where *your* head will be on the block if your group or department fails. Write out the objectives you and your key subordinates have set for each. When convening the next meeting of your group, make three requests of them: First, ask them to restate what you collectively *do not know* that you need to for success. Second, ask them to realize that their job is to think hard and *debate* to reach accurate problem definitions and alternatives for action. Third, ask them to realize you are not seeking consensus, but outstanding results, and that ultimately you must accept the responsibility for making the final decisions based on alternatives they generate.

MY OTHER-CENTEREDNESS INDEX

To determine your *other-centeredness* index, add up your scores from the quizzes listed below. Then mark the rating category that corresponds to your score.

Warmth   _____

Listening   _____

Encouragement   _____

Positive Thinking   _____

Sharing   _____

**My Other-Centeredness
   Index**   _____

                    _____ Superior   22.5–25.0

                    _____ Good   20.0–22.0

                    _____ Satisfactory 17.5–19.5

                    _____ Fair   15.0–17.0

                    _____ Poor   0.0–14.5

II

COURAGEOUS

*There is, in addition to a
courage with which men die,
a courage by which men
must live.*

JOHN F. KENNEDY

IT IS common for us to look to events from military action and famous battles for examples of courage. This is appropriate since no greater enactment of courage can be cited than when a person is willing to risk his life for the sake of others.

However, there are other forms of courage demanded of the peacetime achiever in the executive suite. While the circumstances are not as physically threatening as in warfare, they still involve a formidable emotional risk to the individual, as well as placing his or her career and advancement in jeopardy.

One form of courage characteristic of the executive bent on achievement is to chart and traverse unfamiliar territory. A second is the courage to be oneself, to be the person one is meant to be.

The components of courage for the executive achiever are willingness to: (1) make him or herself vulnerable; (2) speak one's mind fully in a timely fashion; (3) experiment frequently; (4) make bold decisions; and (5) grab hold of his or her unique strengths.

Continue your *achiever development program* by turning to the next chapter and conducting an assessment of your willingness to be vulnerable.

6

Growing Stronger by Being Vulnerable

To test your *vulnerability*, please answer the following questions by marking the response item that most closely matches your typical behavior. Remember, you have everything to gain by being objective in your replies. No one but you will see the results.

1. Is it difficult for you to admit to ignorance on a subject to your associates?
   Usually/Often _____   Sometimes/Seldom _____

2. Do you consider "brainstorming" with your associates a waste of time?
   Usually/Often _____   Sometimes/Seldom _____

3. Do you believe associates think of you as thin-skinned?
   Usually/Often _____   Sometimes/Seldom _____

4. Do you believe your associates think of you as someone who welcomes new ideas?
   Usually/Often _____   Sometimes/Seldom _____

5. Does apologizing to an associate whom you've wronged in some way come easily to you?
   Usually/Often _____   Sometimes/Seldom _____

6. Do you have a confidant or two in your company with whom you share your most candid thoughts and emotions?
   Usually/Often _____   Sometimes/Seldom _____

7. Do you think you have a firm grasp of which associates in

your company should *not* be trusted with your candid thoughts, knowledge of your limitations, and plans for new initiatives?
Usually/Often _____ Sometimes/Seldom _____

8. Are you fearful of being labeled naive, immature, or idealistic when attempting something that hasn't been tried in your company before?
Usually/Often _____ Sometimes/Seldom _____

9. Are you curious? Do you like to play with ideas?
Usually/Often _____ Sometimes/Seldom _____

10. Are you willing to create "a little tension" in your company?
Usually/Often _____ Sometimes/Seldom _____

MY VULNERABILITY INDEX

To determine your score on the *vulnerability* quiz, check your answers against the correct ones listed in Appendix B.

For each correct answer, give yourself one-half point. Add up the correct answers and mark the rating category that corresponds to your score.

My score _____   _____ Superior   4.5–5.0
(Vulnerability Index)   _____ Good   4.0
                           _____ Satisfactory   3.5
                           _____ Fair   3.0
                           _____ Poor   0.0–2.5

BEING VULNERABLE

Most often, we attach a negative value to vulnerability. There are good reasons for this. As stewards of our businesses, we are expected by those who have placed trust in us to devise competitive strategies that obliterate vulnerability. While attaining that ideal isn't possible, we try to keep vulnerability at a minimum in the midst of the ever-present rigors of commerce.

On an individual level, we compete with peers within and outside our companies for career advancement and accomplishment, and go to great lengths to make sure we are not laid bare to those who, given their druthers, would do us in. Then, on a personal level, we plan our estates and provide for our families so as not to find ourselves in dire economic straits later on, or leave our loved ones hurting financially in the event of our death or disability.

Clearly, it seems that only fools knowingly would risk exposing their flanks. Yet there are times when being an achiever demands exactly that. Astute psychologists for a long time have called attention to the fact that most people who are known for their creativity have a childlike quality about them. And it was Jesus who taught his anxious disciples that unless they became like little children they could not reach understanding. I think there is a lesson here. If we can learn to recognize those occasions when we should combine a babe-in-the-woods vulnerability with the right people on the right matters at the right time, we can bring a creative management process to bear on the challenges of business, and achieve distinction rather than mediocrity in working with others.

To Whom

If an intelligent executive willingly makes himself vulnerable, it means he thinks he can make such vulnerability serve some useful purpose. It means he thinks that revealing inadequacies in a given set of circumstances can result in his betterment.

This may seem self-serving, and over the short haul, often is. But it reflects a style that has good portents for the executive and his company over the long haul. Let me give you an example. Recently, I prevailed on a man who is executive vice-president of a large, well-known company to meet me for breakfast. I was doing a search for a corporate client of mine and thought he might make an ideal candidate for the position. I wanted to see if I could induce him to explore this opportunity and, at the same time, take his measure.

This man is a success. His annual income exceeds $400,000; he is considered tops in his discipline; his company would hate to lose him. At one point during our conversation, I asked him what his strengths were. In what ways, I wanted to know, did he stand head and shoulders above his peers. He looked at me, smiled and shook his head. He said, "Boy, that's a tough one. The overall package is pretty good, I guess, but how I stand out, I don't really know." Then he laughed and said, "If you'd asked me about my weaknesses, I could have given you a long list."

Some executives, like this one, come by their vulnerability naturally because their self-esteem is high to begin with. While this particular illustration may not convince everyone that it is representative of this man's day-to-day behavior in the trenches, I would bet that this is the case. It is behavior indicative of a man who is willing to admit to his superiors and subordinates alike when he has made a mistake . . . a person who admits he is bereft of ideas when he is supposed to be a sage; that he blew his stack when he was supposed to be cool as a cucumber; that he was petty when he was supposed to be princely; uninformed when he was supposed to be a seer; timid when he was supposed to be bold; impulsive when he was supposed to watch and wait; and thin-skinned when he was supposed to be confident.

What is essential to keep in mind, however, is that an executive like this one is careful to whom he will reveal his vulnerability. To the best of his judgment, he selects only those associates who will neither violate his trust nor misinterpret the spirit in which he may have conveyed his need for their help, his fear of failure, or shared with them other information that could be used elsewhere in the organization to harm him. Such circumspection is important because being vulnerable always involves taking a risk. If an executive errs in his judgment by making himself vulnerable on the wrong matter or at the wrong time, at least having done so with the right person will reduce the pain and make it short-lived.

About What
Up to now, I have emphasized mainly the kind of vulnerability that is presented in an executive's humanness, foibles, and lesser miscues. While discreetly 'fessing up to these is required of all parties in worthwhile, effective work relations, it also is necessary to expose ourselves to the type of vulnerability that accompanies new initiatives.

This is the type where the act of building something new demands untested measures, and where risk for ruffling feathers runs high. But for fresh, effective action to issue forth on turf that is unfamiliar, what must be present and hold sway is the functioning of a truly open mind. In short, what is needed is a childlike mind: a mind that dares, dreams, is audacious and playful, but is likely to be labeled naive and immature.

This is the game that is worth the candle, *but it can't be played well at the wrong time or without the right sponsors*. It is an irony of organizational behavior that our sponsors are often the ones who provide us with the liberty to embarrass them. That is, they give us a long leash. We can pull on it and create tension, but if we go too far, they can yank us up short and choke us. The trick is to generate a little creative tension, but not pull so hard that we snuff out the opportunities to excel and for them to take pride in us.

In other words, projects where an executive chooses to make him or herself vulnerable by taking bold, new initiatives had better be undertaken only after painstaking consideration of form and content. Nothing is more worth doing; nothing is more rewarding; but the consequences of failure can be devastating. One of the most audacious baseball players of all time was Jackie Robinson. He used to say, "If you're going to steal home, you'd better make it!"

When

When to do what? This is the most critical question when addressing a situation that provides the opportunity for achievement through initiative, but also carries the seeds of defeat. How it is answered in each case determines whether the vulnerability one chooses turns out to be manageable or overwhelming.

The July 13, 1981 *New York Times* carried an article under the headline, "But Can Hollywood Live Without George Lucas?" It was an article that detailed the successes and convictions of this impresario who, in his late twenties and early thirties, has brought us such break-the-mold movies as *American Graffiti, Star Wars, The Empire Strikes Back,* and most recently, *Return of the Jedi.*

Lucas's convictions, which served as the basis for this piece, are his disenchantment with Hollywood and his dreams to have "filmmaking diversified across the country so that every filmmaker isn't locked into thinking the same stale ideas."

The mind-boggling commercial success of his films need not be recounted here. What is important to note, however, is that *Star Wars*, the film that taught America who George Lucas is, stands as one of the most dramatic examples I can generate of bold, fresh initiative undertaken at great risk, both to Lucas and his initial backers. Studios turned down his ideas for the film routinely while scarcely hiding their contempt. Francis Ford Coppola, his mentor and something of an upstart himself, told Lucas his idea was frivolous.

It was precisely the playfulness of *Star Wars* that re-flected the workings of Lucas's mind and sent America on a much-needed foray into fantasy and good times. Though the film appealed to children in droves, I noticed that in the lines outside theaters where the movie was shown, adults also took their places in large numbers.

Obviously, Lucas's timing could not have been better to express his own imagination and capture that of the public. And he demonstrated with repeated successes that his sense and perception in his early movies weren't flukes. Further, he announced his intention to produce a long series of films in the *Star Wars* mode. Though one might suspect his im-pressive sense of timing would dictate that this series be abandoned before completion, it is more likely that it will lead him merely to alter its format in some way to appeal to changing tastes. As one of his associates has said of him, "The vision inside his head is crystal clear. That he cannot be turned from it or be corrupted by outside influences is the key to his success."

Because Lucas made his mark in the field of entertain-ment, where personal performances are paramount, and be-cause he has established a reputation for singular talent and an independent manner, it would be easy to overlook the fact that his success grew out of a management process. That is, he had an idea; it had to be reviewed and tested; it was explored and rejected repeatedly; he had to stand by it and continue to argue persuasively for it; it had to be backed and funded. In the end, it stood up as a viable idea only because several people—not just Lucas—were *willing* to be vulner-able. Several people, no matter what their ages, entered into a gamble with a sense of innocence and risked reputations and dollars; big dollars!

Lucas and his backers were rewarded for having the audacity to try what hadn't been done before. In his coura-geous, tenacious actions, Lucas had found the right people with whom to do the right thing at the right time.

Reports indicate that while he has invested enormous sums to ensure the future of his various enterprises, Lucas's personal tastes and private consumption run to the plain and simple. Though he loves life, he is said to have a sober side.

It is as if Lucas has a long memory for such times as when he came within a hair of death from a car accident at the age of eighteen, and when, on the heels of his hit *American Graffiti*, his follow-up *More American Graffiti* was a flop. It is as if he believes—and all who knowingly would make themselves vulnerable can learn from this—that real achievers never forget their losses.

WRITTEN ACTION PLAN

Suggestions for changing your thought and action to raise your *vulnerability* index.

1. Think of twenty to twenty-five people from among your superiors, peers, and subordinates with whom you're called upon to work closely. Jot their names down as they come to you. After you've completed the list, go back over it and place beside each name either a (+), indicating someone in whom you would confide, or a (0), indicating someone you're not sure of, or a (−), meaning someone in whom you definitely would not confide.

You may find that with added exposure, some people you trust prove not to be worthy of it, while some you don't trust turn out to have been judged unfairly by you. But for a beginning, it is sensible to think through who your allies and opponents are.

2. For a few minutes, forget all barriers that exist for any new initiative you might like to take in your company. Let your mind be playful. Shed your self-consciousness and be your most innocent, childlike, and audacious self. Give your submerged idealism some breathing room and write down five challenging projects that "need doing" for the betterment of the company, and for which you would be the most appropriate catalyst. Let a few days go by, review the list, and select *two* that strike you as doable if certain plausible conditions can be met. Talk these ideas out with two or three people on your peers and subordinates "trust" list.

New initiatives always require approval from on high. If after collaborating with your peers and subordinates, one of your ideas survives, pick a person from your superiors "trust" list and go for it! Try to convince him or her of the merit of your initiative and persuade that person to be your sponsor.

If you fail, repeat the entire process in six months. Mark your calendar.

3. Review your career over the past ten years. Take a sheet of paper and divide it into two columns. On the left, itemize your major successes and, below each, what rewards or gains they brought you. On the right, do the same with your major failures and indicate what penalties or losses they brought you.

On a second sheet of paper, write the actions you took that led to your successes and analyze them to see which ones (with slight modifications) might be repeated in projects and problems you face currently.

On a third sheet, write out the main lessons you have learned from your failures and losses. Ask yourself if any of those lessons, now applied with hindsight, might turn a project or process that in the past was a loser, into a winner today. Moreover, if the lesson learned is timing itself, *this* time might be the *right* time!

7

Executive Discretion:
When to Speak Up,
When to Shut Up

To test your *speaking your mind,* please answer the following questions by marking the response item that most closely matches your typical behavior.

1. Do your associates seek you out for collaboration on projects?
   Usually/Often _____ Sometimes/Seldom _____

2. Do you volunteer your services as a collaborator on projects when you haven't been asked?
   Usually/Often _____ Sometimes/Seldom _____

3. Have you successfully made little-known associates into *supporters* by taking them into your confidence?
   Usually/Often _____ Sometimes/Seldom _____

4. Do you believe your associates think you are too trusting of others?
   Usually/Often _____ Sometimes/Seldom _____

5. Do you believe your associates think you are not trusting *enough* of others?
   Usually/Often _____ Sometimes/Seldom _____

6. Are you willing to be the messenger who brings the bad news to the boss?
   Usually/Often _____ Sometimes/Seldom _____

7. Do you speak your mind without timidity to your bosses when

corporate action is being considered in an area you care about
and in which you have a stake?
Usually/Often _____ Sometimes/Seldom _____

8. Do you speak your opinions prematurely, long before actual
decisions are *made,* in areas you care about deeply?
Usually/Often _____ Sometimes/Seldom _____

9. Do you overglamourize your role and impact on the total
functioning of your corporation?
Usually/Often _____ Sometimes/Seldom _____

10. Do you pick your "battles" carefully?
Usually/Often _____ Sometimes/Seldom _____

MY SPEAKING ONE'S MIND INDEX

To determine your score on the *speaking your mind* quiz, check
your answers against the correct ones listed in Appendix B.

For each correct answer, give yourself one-half point. Add
up the correct answers and mark the rating category that corresponds to your score.

My score _____   _____ Superior   4.5–5.0
(Speaking Your Mind Index)   _____ Good   4.0
                             _____ Satisfactory 3.5
                             _____ Fair   3.0
                             _____ Poor   0.0–2.5

SPEAKING YOUR MIND

Speaking one's mind presents a particular kind of vulnerability. It often is difficult for an executive to know when to speak up and when to shut up. For example, bearing valuable but unwelcome information or opinions risks his being the messenger who brings bad news and has his head chopped off. However, keeping quiet and allowing a decision which would not have been made had his information or views prevailed—even after an explosive or smoldering reception from a touchy superior—risks his being branded a noncontributor or, at least, a timid soul who hasn't the courage to stand up and be counted.

This ever-present damned-if-you-do, damned-if-you-don't dilemma requires extraordinary daily judgment and navigational prowess if an executive is to survive and, more importantly, *thrive* in his or her career.

To Whom

There are three kinds of people in the workplace to whom one can speak his mind freely. The first is those whom he trusts; the second, those he can bring into his trust *by* speaking his mind; and the third, those with whom words may carry less immediate risk, such as his subordinates and suppliers.

Corporations are dependent on key executives being candid with each other when critical issues, problems, and departures are encountered. An example of such a critical time is when a company's major product line is eroding in the marketplace not because of quality problems, but because of service problems whose roots cannot be identified. Another is when a decision needs to be made on completing an acquisition that could make or break the company. Still another is when a new R&D center is under serious consideration to enhance the company's future through strong product development. Such examples demonstrate when ex-

ecutives need to, as Peter Drucker puts it, "pool their ignorance" and weigh alternatives before selecting a course of
action.

While these examples are dramatic in that they require
top management involvement and board approval because
of the large sums of money that are at risk in each case,
corporations are equally dependent on truthful or unfiltered
communications between executives facing operating decisions all the way down the corporate ladder.

What complicates matters, however, is that regardless
of how serious a problem or how great an opportunity a
company faces, all executives have axes to grind and careers
to serve. As a result, not all of us can be trusted at all times.
This is not because we are dishonest, but because we often
are not objective, or our goals simply are in conflict with
those of others. Then too, the personal chemistry or warmth
just may not exist between ourselves and other executives
with whom we have to work. The lobbying, political atmosphere that is inevitable given such undeniable conditions
makes it essential that an executive be extraordinarily discerning before sharing his most candid thoughts with his co-
workers.

Does this sound cynical? It isn't. This simply is a man-
ifestation of the human condition, and my recommendation
for discernment would apply to all organizational spheres
whether of religion, education, government, or voluntary—
wherever people are gathered for a purpose and care about
what happens because they have a stake in events.

Speaking our minds to those we trust needs no comment. Neither does speaking our minds to those where there
is a minimum risk, such as to subordinates and suppliers,
assuming we remain competent and courteous in our work.
But speaking our minds to those *we can bring into our trust*
by doing so does require some comment. This is where powers of discernment are most required of us because speaking
up this way exposes us to vulnerability and risk. But it also

presents great opportunity. By carefully selecting peers, superiors, and sometimes subordinates, with whom we do not have close relationships, but where a sixth sense tells us we may be kindred spirits and hold similar convictions, we have the opportunity—and even the obligation—to link up to make a distinctive contribution to our companies.

These opportunities are presented when pivot points for a company or one of its key functions are reached and controversy surrounds possible corporate action; action in which we and our potential kindred spirits have a stake. This is when we have to shed our timidity and take a stand. These are times when we are called on to be our most persuasive and courageous by voicing our convictions unflinchingly. In short, these are the times that present us with the opportunity to be achievers.

About What
Though daily decisions in a company are important, it is necessary to keep in mind they usually evolve slowly and pertain mostly only to a minuscule facet of a corporation's overall enterprise and risk. So while each decision adds its bit to an entire corporation's functioning and future, an executive never should lose sight of the fact that a decision arrived at in his department or function is just that—a bit. Corporations overcome colossal bad decisions made at the very top by vice-presidents, chief executives, and boards of directors. Acquisitions made that should not have been made— at costs of millions and financed at exorbitant interest rates— are cases in point. The fact that such debacles are overcome should help one to maintain a sense of scale about the decisions on which he has impact. So while his part in operating decisions is serious and important to an executive's career and advancement by virtue of the impression he makes on his superiors, it is not, by itself, *that* crucial to his company. (A *string* of such "bit" decisions may be crucial, but that's another subject.)

Accordingly, whenever one finds himself involved in what influences his company's direction and—no matter how infinitesimally—its future, he must learn to pick his stances and battles carefully. This is the only way to make his "yeas" and "nays" count. If he is outspoken and irascible at every turn, he is asking his co-workers to wonder if he ever has an unexpressed thought! "Tell him all you know Joe, it'll only take a minute," will apply to him. If one must choose between speaking up or shutting up in a given circumstance, it is preferable to abide by the old adage: "Better to remain silent and be thought a fool than to speak and remove all doubt."

Three important questions need to be asked and answered by the executive before he or she elects to take initiative on an issue. The first two are: (1) "Is this something I care about and believe in?" and (2) "Is this an issue or problem to which I can make a distinctive contribution?"

Some executives scatter their efforts and squander their time on concerns that turn out not to be productive for them or their corporations because they have not asked themselves if they *care* about what they're giving themselves to. In other words, they have not made the simple determination or gone through the rudimentary thought process of ascertaining whether or not they are emotionally invested in the issue at hand. If they are not, regardless of how much they tell themselves they *ought* to be, they will find themselves dragging their heels rather than jumping feet first into the fray.

The second question a circumspect executive asks himself before becoming engaged in taking a stand on a controversial course of action is: "Is this an issue or problem or corporate opportunity where I can make good use of my talent?" If an executive has the mental toughness to say to himself and subsequently to others who might want to enlist his services, "Yes, this is a key issue. Yes, this is important to the company, but I think there are better people to address it than I," he then is able to save his time and commitment for situations where his impact can be optimized—to his and the company's benefit.

When

The third question an executive should ask himself when considering his engagement in a corporate issue or problem is: "Is this a good time for me to address this issue?" Speaking up on the right matter in the right way at the right time is what sets the achieving executive apart from the mediocre one. It is tempting to leap into action when an issue or problem one cares about and has a stake in first begins to be bandied about the corporation. However, it usually is premature to do so. Given the fact that most significant decisions concerning a corporation's important activities or new departures are arrived at after much debate and collaboration, one should not take a strong stand during the "trial balloon" stages.

This does not mean an executive ordinarily must give up some of his most prized convictions, but apart from giving voice to his "preliminary view," he should hold his peace until his chances for being heard are optimized. Momentum builds in the decision-making process. There is a time for *discussing* options in which the smart participants to the discussion display flexibility and openness. Then there is the time for *making* the decision. Just before the decision-making crest is reached, the discerning executive who cares deeply about what's at stake speaks his mind in a knowing, balanced manner. He won't win 'em all, but more times than not, he'll carry the day.

WRITTEN ACTION PLAN

Suggestions for changing your thought and action to raise your *speaking your mind* index.

1. Rewrite the names from the first exercise in the last chapter after which you placed a (0). You will remember this indicated persons from the ranks of superiors, peers, and subordinates to whom you're not sure you can extend your trust.

Think hard about these people. Try to put your finger on the source of your suspicions. See if you can justify your doubts by recalling actual events where their actions raised questions in your mind. In some cases, this discipline will provide your answers. But there still will be a few left for whom you will not be able to justify your doubts.

Now call upon your "sixth sense" to choose two or three of these people who you believe would be good collaborators with you in some way if you knew you could be of one accord. *Move toward* these people in the Karen Horney sense. Invite each to lunch, and find other ways to include them in your sphere. Share some of your ideas. Speak some of your opinions, pro and con, on matters with which you're equally familiar. Ask for their ideas and help. Be honest with your responses to what they offer, yet work at seeking common ground. In short, take initiative for establishing fruitful working relationships with these persons.

Not all will respond in the way you might hope, and the exposure might well confirm your earlier suspicions. But in most cases, you'll find your effort well worth making. These are people you can bring into your trust by speaking your mind.

2. List two small projects that need to be done in the company, that you want to see done, that you believe can best be done by you, that can be done quickly, and all you have to do to get approval to do them is fight for them a little.

Do *it* and do *them*.

3. Record five important decisions made by your superiors in the past year that you were a party to and cared about. Put a check mark beside the ones that went the way you wanted them to. If they all did, whatever you're doing, keep it up. Assuming not all did, however, write out and answer these questions for each one that went against you:

○ Was my judgment faulty; were my recommendations wrong?

○ If not, was my timing off; did I present my argument to the final decision maker too early or too late?

○ Was my presentation weak; was I outgunned by the other point of view; was I poorly prepared?

○ Did my argument lack conviction? Did I honestly *not care* about the outcome?

○ Or, was I fearful of stating my point of view even though I had strong convictions?

○ How can I apply what I learn from these answers to my next important (for me) decision-making involvement?

8

The Experimental Commitment:
The Key to Innovative Management

To test your *being experimental,* please answer the following questions by marking the response item that most closely matches your typical behavior.

1. Do you believe your subordinates think you welcome new ideas and initiatives from them?
   Usually/Often _____ Sometimes/Seldom _____

2. Do you make room for the creative "perpetual juvenile" in the department or function you direct?
   Usually/Often _____ Sometimes/Seldom _____

3. Do you encourage yourself and subordinates to ask the "what if . . . ?" and "absurd" questions?
   Usually/Often _____ Sometimes/Seldom _____

4. When you take over a new task or function, are you a practitioner of "change for change's sake"?
   Usually/Often _____ Sometimes/Seldom _____

5. Are you inclined to bring "star performers" who have worked for you in previous departments or companies along with you to your new responsibilities?
   Usually/Often _____ Sometimes/Seldom _____

6. Are you a practitioner of the philosophy, "If it ain't broke, don't fix it?"
   Usually/Often _____ Sometimes/Seldom _____

7. Do you work actively to foster a "feeling of belonging" among your subordinates?
   Usually/Often _____ Sometimes/Seldom _____

8. Do you believe your subordinates think of you as a "things" person rather than a "people" person?
   Usually/Often _____ Sometimes/Seldom _____

9. Do you actively encourage subordinates you consider "high potential" to broaden themselves by leaving your function and moving into another?
   Usually/Often _____ Sometimes/Seldom _____

10. Do you *demand* growth and contribution from your subordinates to the limits of their abilities?
    Usually/Often _____ Sometimes/Seldom _____

MY BEING EXPERIMENTAL INDEX

To determine your score on the *being experimental* quiz, check your answers against the correct ones listed in Appendix B.

For each correct answer, give yourself one-half point. Add up the correct answers and mark the the rating category that corresponds to your score.

My score _____	_____ Superior	4.5–5.0
(Being Experimental Index)	_____ Good	4.0
	_____ Satisfactory	3.5
	_____ Fair	3.0
	_____ Poor	0.0–2.5

BEING EXPERIMENTAL

In 1982, I completed a study* of thirteen major, identified corporations from the three segments of business: consumer, service, and industrial. The study was based on a questionnaire of over 400 items given to 1,086 managers in the 115 headquarters, subsidiaries, and divisions of these corporations. This group was comprised of 515 top and 571 middle management executives. The annual sales of the participating companies ranged from $300 million to $3 billion—a range representative of the largest slice of our gross national product.

The questionnaire was designed to elicit responses from the participating executives in five broad areas: (1) What corporations value; (2) How corporations function; (3) How corporations succeed and fail; (4) What executives are like; and (5) How executives succeed. Given that 93 percent of the executives completed the questionnaire—a task requiring about an hour and a half—I was satisfied that I received valid, representative information in these areas from those who know the corporation best.

While there are abundant instances from the data to show that the American corporation is remarkably robust and worthy of our confidence, there are also some disturbing disclosures that deserve our careful attention and intense remedial efforts. For example:

○ Less than half of the top executives (48 percent) think their corporations give high priority to providing goods and services for society's needs and wants.

○ Less than 10 percent of all executives think their corporations believe in making life less burdensome for the poor in society.

○ Nearly 70 percent of the middle managers think their

*The Cox Report on the American Corporation, Delacorte Press, 1982.

corporations are not staying abreast of needed technology.

o Only half of the top executives think their corporations succeed at adapting to changing market demands; less than 40 percent think they succeed at expanding into and creating *new* markets.

o Less than 30 percent of the middle managers think their companies succeed at expanding international business.

o Less than 40 percent of all executives think their corporations know how to develop general managers.

o Only a fourth of the top executives think "being a student of organizations" is important.

o Only a third of all executives support hiring liberal arts/ humanities majors.

These examples make clear that corporations often experience failure in important matters pertaining to: (1) ideas, (2) methods, and (3) people.

There is a task orientation and division of labor in American corporate life that encourages compartmentalized thinking among executives. There is, of course, a good reason for this. Executives are evaluated in performance by their accomplishment of limited objectives within a narrow focus. This assures the leaders at the top of a large corporation that no one executive or small group can wreak havoc to monstrous proportions. Misdeeds and poor judgments can be confined. This compares with sealing off a fire to a room or corner of a large building.

But there also is a negative tradeoff to this arrangement. The intensity of commitment to the part leads to a lack of coherent thought about the organization as a whole. This further results in isolation and a specialist mentality that leads to being chary of relationships whether they be *thought* relationships or *human* relationships—in or out of the corporation.

While executives of large corporations are very bright, many aren't terribly curious. They don't like to play with ideas as much as some other professionals or executives in smaller companies. Their formidable mental horsepower goes into tactics and short-term, practical problem solving. Most have narrow reading habits and not many read novels with any regularity. They are prodigious workers and their scant leisure time is given to family activities, sports, televiewing, and technical reading. Intellectually speaking, they are not explorers. Few are truly inventive or make good strategists, taking the long view for their corporations. However, those "few" have been and remain crucial to the history and development of the American corporation and society.

Bringing things down to a more personal, individual level, any would-be achiever who has designs on thriving in his or her career in the years ahead has to be able to deal imaginatively with evolutionary change. While corporate planning is necessary to anticipate changes in the marketplace, and personal planning is necessary to anticipate changes in one's career path, what I would call for here is not planning as such, but for an executive to welcome new initiatives and perspectives.

The willingness to welcome such initiatives and perspectives is far less common than corporate and personal rhetoric would lead us to believe. *Change* is invasive, and though we give voice constantly to thriving on it, what we usually mean is that we seek *novelty*, not true change. Change can be wrenching. Who likes to be wrenched?

With Ideas

As I pointed out in chapter 4, it was Alfred North Whitehead who said that everything in the world of thought since Plato has been a footnote. While it may be that in this sense there is nothing new under the sun, the need remains for us to entertain new arrangements and new combinations of existing bodies of thought. For example, the modern age demands that we give up our hyperdependence on cause and effect thinking. More and more, we have learned that the sum of the parts doesn't equal the whole. Sometimes, it is more, sometimes it is less. Though it has become fashionable to say we must not deal with symptoms of problems but rather with their causes, this is not easy to accomplish. A case in point is trying to answer the question, "What causes high interest rates?" Or, "What causes crime?" It seems the answers to such questions only can come from realizing that in some way the parts emerge in anticipation of the whole.

If an executive hopes to deal with change purposefully, he has to be willing to play with ideas. One cannot be rigid if he is to entertain notions that will allow him and his associates to figure out what parts exist in anticipation of what whole.

I mentioned in chapter 6 that psychologists have called attention to the fact that truly creative people have a child-like quality about them. This quality causes some people to write them off as immature. Most great companies grew out of a single sound idea that was given birth to and nurtured by an entrepreneur so committed to it that he usually was considered arbitrary and petulant. What is most fascinating about such characters in American business history, however, is that they had not just one great idea, but were so inclined that they seldom stopped having them. They continued to feed their enterprises with their imagination.

The late Eric Hoffer wrote penetratingly about such people and distinguishes them from the revolutionaries who erroneously are believed by the naive to be creative. He says, "Both the revolutionary and the creative individual are perpetual juveniles. The revolutionary does not grow up because he cannot grow while the creative individual cannot grow up because he keeps growing."

With Methods

Federal Express has been a stirring growth company. It bolted out of the blue and became the fine gem of the air freight business. The company developed a reputation for being quick, adaptable, and reliable. Any traveler crisscrossing the nation can't miss their ubiquitous diesel pickup and delivery vans in the business centers in all major cities of America.

This company achieved such rapid success because it has a top management that insists on infusing its organization with the belief in experimenting with methods. Its management went so far as to consider employing blimps to transport its freight. The idea was rejected in the end but shows that the company is not afraid to ask the all-important "What if . . . ?" questions. "Given the fuel shortage and attendant rising costs, what if we used blimps?" is not an absurd question, even though it might seem so. Executives need to ask such questions, and go even further and ask absurd ones. For example, "What if water ran uphill? How would that change things? How would that affect our business?"

The Chicago River is famous in the annals of civil engineering. This isn't because it runs uphill, but because in 1900, after eight years of toil and the completion of an intricately designed system of locks, its flow was reversed to benefit Chicago's citizens. This reversal was sought to reduce death rates from disease caused by sewage flowing from the river into Lake Michigan, the source of the city's drinking water. In 1854, 5 percent of the city's population died from cholera. In 1891, long before A. J. Liebling tagged it so, Chicago claimed the untoward distinction of being the second city, that is, in the rate of death from typhoid fever.

With the reversal of the flow of the river away from Lake Michigan these killer diseases were eliminated. However, thinking back to the 1800s, we have to give credit to the lonely soul who first asked if this busy port river running through the center of town could be made to defy the laws of nature. Whoever he was, he was a hero. But I think it likely that at the time he posed his critical question, he was considered by most of his listeners to be a fool.

Another way executives are called upon to be experimental—but often fail at it—is by experimenting with methods they inherit from predecessors. Most executives like to put their stamp on matters when they take over a new job. They immediately rush to reorganize, revamp, and redeploy. In the press to show they are people of action, they feel compelled to make changes in the way things are done. They are quick to claim they were brought in to improve circumstances surrounding the job. Actually, the newly promoted executive should bear one thing in mind: despite his superiors telling him they're counting on improvements, his predecessor might have been promoted because of his or her excellence and the bosses may hope merely that the new incumbent will be able to maintain the status quo.

When John Welch became chief executive of General Electric in 1981, he waited several months before even rearranging the furniture in the office he inherited from Reginald Jones. This caused quite a stir because it was such a jarring contrast to what usually happens when "the new man takes over." The maxim, "If it ain't broke, don't fix it," is one Welch adheres to tenaciously. (On the other hand, he moves quickly to fix what *is* broke.)*

My work requires that I interview and evaluate executives for top management positions. During some of these interviews, the people sitting across from me may begin to

---

*Ironically, in the fall of 1984, some time after writing this chapter, I came across a copy of a speech by John Welch in which he took issue with the "If it ain't broke, don't fix it" point of view. Then the October 1, 1984 *Wall Street Journal* carried a full page ad by General Electric under the headline, "If it ain't broke, fix it." This attitude and implicit management command emanating from corporate headquarters is a no doubt sincere but unfortunate departure from Welch's earlier days on the new job. In my opinion, this directive is likely to be ignored (though given lip service) by many GE operating managers, and taken by others to be an invitation to meddle needlessly, and, in some cases, harmfully. I do not expect it to persist as dogma in this great company.

elaborate on how they would be eager to take on the challenge of the job and that they have several members of their current management team they would bring with them because they are such "stars." These conversations always make me nervous and lead me to wonder if these executives are far too dependent on their "traveling support group." They often seem to be persons who want to impose tired, routine methods with which they are comfortable on a new corporate culture where those methods will be inappropriate and ill-fitting.

The real test for an executive is to be experimental with existing methods. True enough, the time for changing them may come, but the confident executive will use the resources that already exist to put new wine into old wineskins. On this topic Hoffer again was instructive: "A true talent will make do with any technique."

With People

Simply put, the primary day-to-day challenge facing all corporations is providing a feeling of belonging for their people. Providing this feeling of belonging may be thought of as manipulation by the so-called hard-noses in the executive suite. They see it as a euphemism for pacifying lower levels of management and workers in order to get them to buy into the company "program." What these hard-noses don't recognize is their own lack of feeling of belonging. In short, they feel out of place in the factory, and consider the company picnic (if they even consent to have one) a chore. Just give them their computer printouts, financial reports, antiseptic offices, and three-piece suits.

This state of affairs merely symbolizes that where their people are concerned, such managements are bereft of imagination and a sense of experimentation. These managements are made up predominantly of "things" persons rather than "people" persons. Their successes, whatever they may be, will be short-lived. "Things" persons who occupy executive positions are individuals who look at their co-workers and themselves in a mechanistic way. They see themselves as bossing and being bossed with little regard for human potential and a sense of kinship in their managerial exchanges.

It is becoming more widely known that corporations are notoriously poor at preparing their younger executives for general management responsibilities. Part of the problem stems from the natural tendency to overexpose executives to one function without adequate training in others. A marketing executive tends to come of age not knowing enough about finance; a finance executive tends to reach his peak without knowing enough about manufacturing; a manufacturing executive may be emotionally ready for a major profit-and-loss responsibility, but lacks adequate knowledge of personnel and organizational issues.

This overspecialization shows that while companies are adept at bringing executives along well in their main fields, they are not experimental enough with them by assuming and providing for their competence in other functions. Put another way, corporations maximize the short-term contributions of the executives while putting a cap on their long-term growth and contribution. As a result of less than imaginative utilization of their potential management resources, corporations often have to recruit from the outside when they have a need for an executive to fill a general management position. This occurs after they survey their inventory of managers and conclude they don't have anyone in-house who is truly "ready."

Of course some companies are relatively new and grow so fast that they never are quite able to keep up with their need for key management. Unlike the situation I've just described, going to the outside here does not harm morale because expansion creates room for everyone to grow and be fully challenged to make their optimum contribution.

It is inevitable that from time to time you will need to ask yourself to what extent you have contributed to a sub-

ordinate's being one-dimensional. Then you need to ask yourself if he truly is one-dimensional or just demoralized; grown
stale in a function because you haven't *demanded* growth and
contribution from him. There is a good rule of thumb for
promoting or moving a subordinate into what is unfamiliar
territory for him. That is, if you think he just might pull it
off, go ahead and put him into it despite your doubts. The
chances are that he will surprise you by making good.

WRITTEN ACTION PLAN

Suggestions for changing your thought and action to raise
your *being experimental* index.

1. Develop an idea-generating discipline *that is not directly
related to your work.* Here's how: Be sure to read some good
fiction for its humanizing effects. Always keep a book and a
magazine or two in your briefcase for when you travel. I've
got nothing against Robert Ludlum (he's great for an occa-
sional escape), but you can have better companions than his
books to feed your mind while facing airplane delays and
being aboard long flights.

Include nonfiction in your program as well A good source
for recommending titles is Edmund Fuller's column in *The
Wall Street Journal.* His reviews offer excellent insight into
many good books full of good ideas. In addition to a general
news magazine, subscribe to a publication you think of as
not relevant to you. Good examples are *Rolling Stone* and
Mad Magazine. Both will school you about the future in ways
your business and associates never will.

Keep televiewing to a minimum. In particular, don't
stay glued to the tube passively watching sports events each
weekend. Rather, attend a movie, or a play, or a lecture, or
join a discussion-study group. Talk over plots and characters
with your spouse and children, and explore and *feel* what an
artist is saying about life through his music, sculpture, and
painting.

Write out the details for executing your idea-generating discipline, review it monthly, and begin reading your first work of fiction this week. An executive's mind is often one-track and harried—one to which a good idea has difficulty gaining entrance. On the other hand, a *varied* mind is adaptable and receptive to applicable ideas sprung from unlikely sources.

2. Consider your current job and responsibilities. Think of the segments you inherited from your predecessors that have a "sacred cow" aura about them. They might include such items as, "We *always* have held the annual sales conference at Marco Island," or "We use *only* Baker sprockets on our machines," or "Nobody can be a top executive in *this* retail company unless he or she has run one of our stores."

List all these sacred cows and put a check mark next to those that can be left alone for now. "If it ain't broke, don't fix it."

Given the demands on your time, and seeking to do first things first, address those you didn't mark, eliciting ideas from your subordinates on how you jointly can embark on *new initiatives* without violating *old forms*.

3. Write down all the names of the subordinates who report directly to you. Place a check mark next to anyone you consider one-dimensional. Before giving in to the temptation to believe that person lacks ambition or verve, ask yourself if you've made clear that you expect to see an *appetite* in him or her for professional and personal growth. Also ask yourself if your company and department rigidly pigeonhole people, with the result that broadening exposures are difficult to obtain.

If you remain convinced the problems of arrested growth lie within the individual, discuss a growth program with him or her privately and state that "the train's moving and it's time to get on or off."

9

Making Bold Decisions:
Learning When to Say "Yes," "No,"
and "Wait"

MAKING BOLD DECISIONS QUIZ

To test your *making bold decisions,* please answer the following
questions by marking the response item that most closely matches
your typical behavior.

1. Do you avoid making "yes" decisions?
   Usually/Often _____ Sometimes/Seldom _____

2. Do you avoid making "no" decisions?
   Usually/Often _____ Sometimes/Seldom _____

3. Do you avoid making "that's gonna have to wait" decisions?
   Usually/Often _____ Sometimes/Seldom _____

4. Do you make "wait" decisions *quickly?*
   Usually/Often _____ Sometimes/Seldom _____

5. Boldness in saying "no" may well "go against the grain" in
   your corporation at a given time; when there's a rush to "do
   something," are you willing to take the heat?
   Usually/Often _____ Sometimes/Seldom _____

6. Do you show discernment in decision making by spotting and
   labeling "group-think," "fashion," and "wishful thinking"
   among your subordinates who are jointly grappling with a
   problem?
   Usually/Often _____ Sometimes/Seldom _____

7. Do you use your decision making as a training and devel-

opment opportunity for your subordinates? Do you meet with them to explain your reasoning and the tradeoffs you faced in reaching decisions?

Usually/Often _____ Sometimes/Seldom _____

8. Do you put off making decisions because you fear being wrong?

Usually/Often _____ Sometimes/Seldom _____

9. Are you annoyed that your subordinates want decisions from you on their recommendations too quickly?

Usually/Often _____ Sometimes/Seldom _____

10. Have you rebounded quickly from decisions you've made that in hindsight have proved to be wrong?

Usually/Often _____ Sometimes/Seldom _____

MY MAKING BOLD DECISIONS INDEX

To determine your score on the *making bold decisions* quiz, check your answers against the correct ones listed in Appendix B.

For each correct answer, give yourself one-half point. Add up the correct answers and mark the rating category that corresponds to your score.

My score _____   _____ Superior   4.5–5.0
(Making Bold Decisions   _____ Good   4.0
Index)   _____ Satisfactory   3.5
                           _____ Fair   3.0
                           _____ Poor   0.0–2.5

MAKING BOLD DECISIONS

Being a good decision maker is one of the clichéd requirements for being an achiever. In the recitations of those who
know best what makes for managerial effectiveness, there is
no doubt that if one waffles in making decisions, or makes
bad ones repeatedly, he or she will not enjoy success in a top
executive business career.

Clearly, then, there is little room for debate that a minimum of decision-making ability is a necessity for a modicum
of executive success. Moreover, it also is clear that some
executives are better decision makers than others, and that
all executives make better decisions at certain times than
they do at others. Therefore, among the truly important matters in considering excellence of management are the *quality*
of decisions and the *consistency* of quality decisions made
by executives.

An ingredient critical to quality decision making is boldness. The courage to take steps that shake an enterprise out
of its lethargy, or block a headlong rush that seems *so* obviously indicated by all of one's associates up, down, and
across the organization, is a personal trait that has been and
remains rare among all groups, and no less so in the ranks
of corporate management.

In addressing boldness in decision making, it is essential
to see its part in three kinds of decisions: (1) *Yes* decisions,
(2) *No* decisions, and (3) *Wait* decisions. When made properly,
all three release initiative.

Yes Decisions
By their natures some executives are more inclined than
others to say "yes" to ideas, proposals, inquiries, and actions.
Their opposite number, for the same reasons of nature and
personal development, find it easier to say "no." Still others,
more inclined to a hesitating approach to life, are most comfortable saying "wait." Yet for an executive to function fully

and capably, it is necessary to rise above his or her inclinations and say all three words at different times depending on circumstances.

A "yes" decision maker is not a yes-man. For example, all great companies began with a big yes because the initial step taken by the founder acting on an idea is an overwhelming affirmative action. And anyone who has spent time with entrepreneurs knows they are among the most determined creatures on the planet, not at all given to waffling.

Further, all great companies continue growing because they have mastered the art (and sometimes the science) of saying yes to the right ideas and actions. This is courageous because saying yes always entails risk. Invariably, it requires an enormous investment of funds, people, and time. If that investment shows itself to have been made in vain, the company may fail, its record may be marred, its stock price may be assaulted, earnings may falter, or careers may suffer.

Nonetheless, if an executive in a key position is not committed to say yes to launching a new product, building a new plant, hiring or promoting an extraordinary subordinate, buying state-of-the-art equipment and machinery, experimenting with organization structure and functioning, acquiring a company in an imaginative way, or somehow betting on the future, he or she will not be contributing to the company what it has every right to expect. Unless that executive works for a company in slow decline, his or her play-it-safe career eventually will come a cropper.

The traditional thinking about line and staff jobs is well founded. This is particularly so if you think of the people who hold staff jobs as *recommenders* and the holders of line jobs as *deciders*. Some people just aren't comfortable (despite their protestations to the contrary) making decisions, and do not belong in "the buck stops here" line jobs. On the other hand, they may possess brilliance or keen analytical abilities the deciders lack.

In order for corporate decisions to be made and made

wisely, it is desirable that decision-making jobs be occupied
by deciders, not recommenders. Further, it is even more critical that this be the case when the decisions required by a
company are yes decisions. All executives, including staff
executives, make decisions. All executives recommend to their
superiors and receive recommendations from subordinates.
But it is the line executive whose decisions have a direct
impact on profit (or lack of it) and whose position gives rise
to the expression, "His job is on the line."

Line and staff designations get hazy, to say the least, at
top management levels if we direct our attention to the strange
animal called *group vice-president*. The group VP is a coach,
not a quarterback. He is a question asker and direction setter
(coach) for his division presidents or general managers
(quarterbacks). Technically, this makes him staff, because
the division heads are making the line operating decisions
for their businesses. Yet this role, an invention of the modern,
complex corporation, is great training for its incumbent, who
usually *was* a line jobholder and now functions as a superior
in the collaborative mode essential to management 1980s
style. His job is to *inspire* the right yes decisions from his
subordinates.

No Decisions

The trap of saying no is that it seemingly avoids risk. It can
lull the decision maker into breathing a sigh of relief over
another wrong turn having been passed. The *comfort* of averting mistakes is much more appealing than the *anxiety* of
going after victories that always can turn out to be elusive.
"It is better to do nothing on a small scale than fail on a big
one," goes such subterranean thinking.

Of course, the real risk with this kind of thinking is that
it can lead to self-deception with the long-term result of corporate demise over failure of nerve. This is what is at stake
and constitutes "Bet Your Company" in a context where we
seldom hear this phrase used.

Having sounded this cautionary note, I hastily add that

a would-be decision maker who will not say no is headed for disaster. Such an executive will show him or herself to be lacking, first of all, discernment; second, a sense of steward-ship of a company's financial and human resources; and third, self-confidence. To achieve over the long pull and win the respect of associates, an executive must be able to say no boldly.

A superior's boldness in saying no is called for in those frequent cases where there is a need to go against the grain of his subordinates. Numerous situations arise in business and the essential management collaborations that produce a sort of *group-think* among participants where "everybody" involved just "knows" that "this" (whatever has caught their fancy) is the "only" way to go.

Not necessarily so! At least not to the superior with discernment, a sense of stewardship, and self-confidence. This superior is not disposed to conform to the "fashions" cours-ing through the ranks of "progressive" managements else-where, nor is he swayed by the contorted logic of his subordinates collectively caught up in their own rhetoric and wishful thinking as they grapple with a frustrating problem.

The two most important purposes served by judiciously saying no are: (1) to help assure the long-term success of one's company; and (2) to contribute to the development of one's subordinates. By discerningly saying no and carefully stating the reasons for it, the superior is a model and teacher for all subordinates. Further, the subordinates are free to take initiative on more productive projects now that the one under consideration has been put to bed.

Wait Decisions

It is destructive for subordinates to be kept waiting for a decision that isn't being made because a superior is timid. However, a superior waiting to make a decision because he concludes the time is not right to deal with an issue is being bold. For this, too, often goes against the grain.

My studies of almost 1,100 top and mid-level executives

in thirteen major corporations revealed that out of a long list of workstyle options, quick decision making is the most preferred behavior. Seventy-four percent top executives and 67 percent middle indicate that their corporations encourage such decision making. If a superior is going to say "wait," it helps to say so quickly.

Of course the critical factor in deciding to wait is not the passing of time itself, but the proper exercise of judgment. Postponing action until a more appropriate time—or when circumstances indicate such action should not be taken at all—is the mark of an executive who won't be seduced by the corporate lure to be a fast gun.

While subordinates invariably want and have a right to expect prompt responses to their recommendations, there's no denying that these recommendations deserve careful thought and the optimum time and method for putting them into place. Among the 1,100 executives mentioned earlier, 62 percent top and 57 percent middle say that good judgment has a very positive impact on their careers. Thirty-seven percent top and 40 percent middle say good judgment has a somewhat positive impact on their careers.

To the eager subordinate who is asked to generate information and recommendations quickly, a fast wait from the boss may not seem fair reward. Yet it is the more mature of these subordinates who realize that an ill-timed good idea is misspent initiative. And the boss can use these decision-making crossroads as a training ground and test track to see how his or her juniors respond to and adapt to choices adverse to their druthers, and the wisdom of which they cannot see.

One last item needs to be kept in mind. That is, the boss won't always be right. It well may be that the subordinate has been right by recommending no, but the boss boldly says yes; or the subordinate recommends now, but the boss boldly decides wait. Nonetheless, the boss who excels is the one who has reached a level of achievement because of being right more than wrong, and being bold in making key decisions. It is no accident that this is the kind of boss who wins the respect of quality subordinates over time and shows him or herself to be a rare developer of young executive talent.

WRITTEN ACTION PLAN

Suggestions for changing your thought and action to raise your *making bold decisions* index.

1. Think about yourself a few moments and write down whether, by inclination, you are mostly a "yes," "no," or "wait" decision maker. Write out ten important decisions you've made over the past year, and beside each indicate whether it was a "yes," "no," or "wait" decision. Further, beside each "wait" decision, if enough time has elapsed, indicate whether that "wait" became "yes" or "no."

If, for example, you think of yourself as a "yes" decision maker, but most of the decisions you made turned out to be "no" or "wait," you need to evaluate whether your self-assessment is accurate, or if circumstances themselves are responsible for these decisions contrary to your inclination.

It is important to know your inclination so you can act naturally on it, but also so you can be on guard against relying on it without proper discernment. Therefore, if you remain unsure of your leanings, repeat the above exercise for the prior year.

2. Think about your boss for a few moments and write down whether, by inclination, she or he is mostly a "yes," "no," or "wait" decision maker.

Write out ten important decisions your boss has made over the past year. Beside each, indicate whether it was a "yes," "no," or "wait" decision. Beside each "wait" decision, if enough time has elapsed, further indicate whether that "wait" became "yes" or "no."

Does the tally square with your assessment? If you're not sure, repeat the exercise for the prior year. It is important to know your boss's inclination, first of all, so you can tailor your work and presentations to please her or him. Second, when you may be heading for disagreement, you won't be flying blind trying to design a proposal that will overcome her or his objections.

Carefully review your written action plan for exercise number 3 in chapter 7, "Executive Discretion: When to Speak Up, When to Shut Up."

3. Write out whether you most enjoy *making* profit decisions or *recommending* them. Being brutally honest with yourself on this point will go a long way toward helping you determine what kind of long-range career you should seek and positions you should try to occupy.

10

How to Act on Your Unique Strengths

ACTING ON YOUR UNIQUE STRENGTHS QUIZ

To test your *acting on your unique strengths,* please answer the following questions by marking the response item that most closely matches your typical behavior.

1. Do you rely too much on your "commodity" or "me too" strengths for your day-to-day performance?
   Usually/Often _____   Sometimes/Seldom _____

2. Do you *savor* your "flashes" of insight and commitment?
   Usually/Often _____   Sometimes/Seldom _____

3. Do you follow up those flashes with planning and hard work?
   Usually/Often _____   Sometimes/Seldom _____

4. Do you view your work with your associates as what you owe of *yourself* to a community of people?
   Usually/Often _____   Sometimes/Seldom _____

5. Do you give hard thought to the ways in which you are like *no other person?*
   Usually/Often _____   Sometimes/Seldom _____

6. Do you determine in what areas of your company that superior performance by you will have the most impact?
   Usually/Often _____   Sometimes/Seldom _____

7. Do you feel bogged down by the "bureaucracy" in your company?
   Usually/Often _____   Sometimes/Seldom _____

8. Do you face your job with a task-force mentality?
Usually/Often _____   Sometimes/Seldom _____

9. Do you plan too much, act too little?
Usually/Often _____   Sometimes/Seldom _____

10. Does the urging from your boss to "do it now!" send chills up and down your spine?
Usually/Often _____   Sometimes/Seldom _____

MY ACTING ON YOUR UNIQUE STRENGTHS INDEX

To determine your score on the *acting on your unique strengths* quiz, check your answers against the correct ones listed in Appendix B.

For each correct answer, give yourself one-half point. Add up the correct answers and mark the rating category that corresponds to your score.

My score _____   _____ Superior   4.5–5.0
(Acting on Your Unique   _____ Good   4.0
Strengths Index)   _____ Satisfactory   3.5
                              _____ Fair   3.0
                              _____ Poor   0.0–2.5

ACTING ON YOUR UNIQUE STRENGTHS

It was Henri Bergson who admonished us to engage two critical ingredients in order to bring about distinctive accomplishments in our lives. His straightforward directive was: "Think like a man of action, act like a man of thought." There is no better advice for any woman or man to follow anywhere, anytime.

The world is full of unreflective actors and inactive thinkers. While the former may cause us disaster in a hurry, the latter deny us the benefits of their thoughts because of their passivity. Both have their place at times, it's true. Emergencies arise and are often dealt with effectively by those who rush in where angels fear to tread. Moreover, the early Greek philosophers made clear that the leisure class was necessary to the birth of great ideas.

However, given the ordinary nature of most of our lives as executives, we typically are not beset with emergencies, nor are most of us members of what the Greeks thought of as the leisure class. We work hard and long. The trick is to work smart. In other words, to think well before we act. But act we must, in a timely fashion, in a prudent way, making use of our unique strengths in a set of circumstances—no matter what they are—viewed with what opportunities they present as well as what barriers they throw in our way.

Unique Strengths

We have a pretty good handle on our basic strengths. We also are good at using them. They are what could be called our professional credentials and include our education and training, experience, and broad aptitudes. For the most part, these strengths got us where we are.

Essential as these strengths are to functioning well, they are not our most important ones. We could say that among the energetic and ambitious with any vision of the future, they are *commodity* strengths—necessary, but taken for granted and not distinguishing in any salient way.

The strengths that are unique, that we all possess in ample measure and are ours alone, are the ones that set us apart on our jobs and in our performance. These are the strengths that reside in our individually developed senses of caring and clarity and cultivating our initiative and special talents. While our being professionals means we sometimes will do craftsmanlike work when we least feel like it, it is our unique strengths that enable us to soar; to produce that head-turning accomplishment. The late Eric Hoffer wrote: "That which is unique and worthwhile in us makes itself felt in flashes. Unless we know how to catch and savor the flashes, we are without growth and without exhilaration."

Catching the flashes means to act on them. It means to take initiative, rather than letting them pass and adding to the buildup of discouragement within our spirits. One doesn't soar daily, however. By definition, flashes aren't commonplace. But changes and challenges in business and corporate life come often enough and are pressing enough that flashes, which materialize in the form of fresh approaches, are cheered.

The flash comes first; the hard work follows. The important thing to keep in mind is that the flash—which ordinarily doesn't arrive in cosmic splendor, but simply wafts onto a mind that is willing to be playful with ideas and alive to what it *cares* about—gives firepower to the labors that inevitably lie ahead in *achieving practical results*.

To repeat what I said in the Introduction to this book, we seem to have entered a particularly good time in American business life. Given the currency of the term "corporate culture," I choose to call this new attitude the "culture of caring." For a corporation to thrive, to be profitable enough to attract continued investment, it has to do two things. First, it has to create the feeling of belonging among all its people; second, it has to maintain an intense relationship with its customers. After World War II, we taught the Japanese how these work to benefit and then promptly forgot our own lessons, with the result that they have outperformed us by applying this rudimentary knowledge for the past fifteen years.

It is gratifying that corporate America is awake again. The culture of caring calls for and rewards executives who, rather than being somnambulists offering run-of-the-mill skills and a financial harvesting bias, are uncompromising about acting on their unique strengths. This is the stuff of achievers.

Reading the Stream

It is well known that we do not give expression to our unique strengths in a vacuum. Alas, there is always the context. For executives, that translates to the corporate organization and its particular environment—the marketplace and society-at-large on a worldwide basis. To make our unique strengths truly useful to our corporations, it is essential that we become skillful in understanding that context. In short, we need to know how to read the stream.

It is a pleasant paradox in human nature that we are uniquely and most distinctively ourselves when we are participating members of a group enterprise or activity. In other words, our true individuality is expressed when we are called upon to make a contribution to a group or "community." Further, when we fail to do so, it becomes clear to all, including ourselves, that we aren't carrying our weight. It is in intense collective interactions that we partake of the important wisdom of how we are like *all* other people, how we are like *some* other people, and how we are like *no* other person. Every management group or team is made up of individuals who share these commonalities and differences, and their particular mixture determines the degree of competition and cooperation that exist in it.

Reading the stream in a corporation means that an achieving executive is discerning in choosing those areas of activity and the departments in a corporation where he or she has the best chance of making a maximum, distinctive contribution. He or she looks around and asks, "What does this company want accomplished?" (The answer won't come from pat rhetoric. Remember that corporations often are not good at articulating their real goals.) Then the achiever asks, "In what area and group will superior performance by me produce the most impact?" Last, he or she asks, "In tandem with which people am I most likely to excel?"

You may think I am calling for more autonomy on the part of executives than corporate structures allow. Your thought may be that one is *placed* in a department or division with a specific set of tasks outlined in some job description. While I agree that corporate structure must be served (and will treat this subject in some detail in Appendix A), we have a great deal more freedom to create initiatives and alliances to accomplish our defined responsibilities than we often realize. Moreover, those initiatives are far more appreciated by superiors than we're inclined to think.

What is necessary to act autonomously is for us to face our jobs with a *task-force mentality*. This provides experimental thought, collaborations and the testing of ideas, the reward of joint effort, and accommodates the need to abandon quickly the organizational alliances and mechanisms when the task at hand is completed. One and all can then get on with other, pressing concerns.

By joining or assembling a group that is thought of as a task force—even though not formally labeled as such—the executive wisely signs on where he gives what is valued and what he values is, in turn, given. He sees to it that he has an impact. This is not marching to the beat of a different drummer. Rather, it is drumming the beat to different marchers.

Acting Now

Earlier, I said that careful thought should precede action. The achiever plans his work, then *works* his plan. One of the hazards of planning is that it can be so alluring an exercise that it substitutes for actions. Forever preparing ourselves, we sometimes never quite get around to delivering the goods. Under such circumstances, the chances are good that we are avoiding action where we question our ability to perform well.

While postponing action in the name of planning or some other ruse is human enough, and characteristic of all of us more than we might like to admit, it is overcoming this timidity that leads to worthwhile achievement. True to the perversity of human nature, it seems that the challenges that frighten us the most are precisely those that prove exhilarating when we lower our heads and gut them through.

What executive does not now and then dream of glory? Yet more often than not does not the dream entail the executive's turning in a stellar performance making use of unique strengths that he knows he possesses, but is afraid to employ in real life? The deception that he may then engage in is, "Well, the time's not right, but one of these days . . ."

Well, the time is right, and it's *now*. Like the placard says, *Do it now!* Whether what needs to be done is a one-shot thrust and can be taken care of immediately, or a journey of a thousand miles that begins with the first step, the time to act must not be postponed. *Now* is of the essence.

Taking action on your unique strengths, when down below your knees are knocking, is courageous action. It may mean offending others whose interests are different from yours, and having to perform when all about you seems thrown into chaos by the moves you make. Yet it is taking such action that distinguishes the achiever from the also-rans.

Pop folk singer and composer Gordon Lightfoot catches this idea intriguingly in his song *Race Among the Ruins*:

> When you wake up to the promise
> of your dream world comin' true
> with one less friend to call on
> was it someone that I knew?
> Away you will go sailing

in a race among the ruins
if you plan to face tomorrow
do it soon.

Now is soon enough.

WRITTEN ACTION PLAN

Suggestions for changing your thought and action to raise your *acting on your unique strengths* index.

1. List twenty ways you are like all other people. Then list fifteen ways you are like some other people. Then list ten ways you are like no other person.

2. Ruminate a bit. Put your feet up. Recall three or four "flashes" you had in the past three years but failed to follow up on. Write them down. Did they not—no matter in how small a measure—involve your employing unique strengths you know you possess, but are for some reason afraid to act on at work?

Write down five unique strengths you have but have kept hidden from others and are afraid to act on. Carefully satisfy yourself for each one if you would really *like* to act on it. For those where you would, grab hold of them. Own them! Say *Yes, Yes, Yes* to yourself.

3. Determine *today* that you are not going to be a somnambulist offering run-of-the-mill skills. You are not going to be merely a planner, but also a doer. You, in your small way, are going to drum the beat to different marchers. You are going to contribute to the *culture of caring*. You now have the natural firepower for the hard work that lies ahead.

Begin by writing out three questions:

(a) What does my company want accomplished? Give five answers.

(b) In what area and group will superior performance by me produce the most impact? Give no more than two answers.

(c) In tandem with which people am I most likely to excel? List four to six names.

You now know what, where, why, and with whom. You also know when: *Now*! The how will come later.

MY COURAGE INDEX

To determine your *courage* index, add up your scores from the quizzes listed below. Then mark the rating category that corresponds to your score.

Vulnerability   _____

Speaking Your Mind   _____

Experimentation .   _____

Making Bold Decisions   _____

Acting on Unique Strengths   _____

My Courage Index   _____

_____ Superior   22.5–25.0

_____ Good   20.0–22.0

_____ Satisfactory 17.5–19.5

_____ Fair   15.0–17.0

_____ Poor   0.0–14.5

III

JUDICIOUS

The world stands aside to let anyone pass who knows what he is doing.

DAVID STARR JORDAN

OF THE FOUR broad qualities making up the profile of the achiever, I find *judicious* the most difficult to capture in writing. Surely this isn't because it is more intangible than the other three. Indeed, they are all equally intangible.

Rather I suspect the difficulty I experience with writing about good judgment is because it is more *inclusive*. That is, if an executive is characterized by good judgment, he will think and do most of what is necessary to be an achiever. In other words, if he has good judgment, he will be other-centered, courageous, and resourceful. He will be these "things" because they are what is called for; they bring appropriate results. On the other hand, an executive may be other-centered, courageous, and resourceful at various times without being judicious.

These latter comments remind me of one of the first lessons from Miss Curtis in my fifth-grade math class. It was: All squares are rectangles, but all rectangles aren't squares. The message from this lesson was that while squares are worthy of our special attention, rectangles are a more complex subject. So it is with good judgment when discussing the achiever.

Enough said. The signs of good judgment are these: (1) making judicious decisions; (2) setting priorities; (3) being tenacious; (4) having a sense of humor; and (5) making one's own luck.

Continue your *achiever development program* by conducting an assessment of your judgment in making decisions.

11

Making Judicious Decisions:
How Foresight Matches Hindsight

To test your *making judicious decisions,* please answer the following questions by marking the response item that most closely matches your typical behavior. Remember, you have everything to gain by being objective in your replies. No one but you will see the results.

1. Do you ask yourself what is the most important decision you should make *now?*
   Usually/Often _____ Sometimes/Seldom _____

2. Do you postpone decisions that should be made *now?*
   Usually/Often _____ Sometimes/Seldom _____

3. Do you second-guess your decisions?
   Usually/Often _____ Sometimes/Seldom _____

4. Does hindsight show your decisions to have been the right ones?
   Usually/Often _____ Sometimes/Seldom _____

5. Do you maintain an animated, inquiring, processing mind?
   Usually/Often _____ Sometimes/Seldom _____

6. Do you avoid listening to your "inner voice" when making decisions?
   Usually/Often _____ Sometimes/Seldom _____

7. Do you listen to your "inner voice" to learn what you *care* about deep down?
   Usually/Often _____ Sometimes/Seldom _____

8. Do you "inflate" the importance of your decisions?
Usually/Often _____ Sometimes/Seldom _____

9. Do you look carefully at the "little" decisions you and your company make as signs that tell you where you and your company are headed?
Usually/Often _____ Sometimes/Seldom _____

10. Have the "big decisions" you've made added to your self-esteem?
Usually/Often _____ Sometimes/Seldom _____

MY MAKING JUDICIOUS DECISIONS INDEX

To determine your score on the *making judicious decisions* quiz, check your answers against the correct ones listed in Appendix B.

For each correct answer, give yourself one-half point. Add up the correct answers and mark the rating category that corresponds to your score.

My score _____		
(Making Judicious Decisions	_____ Superior	4.5–5.0
Index)	_____ Good	4.0
	_____ Satisfactory	3.5
	_____ Fair	3.0
	_____ Poor	0.0–2.5

MAKING JUDICIOUS DECISIONS

The confidence to make decisions is what separates the women from the girls. Success in making *judicious* decisions is what separates achievers from nonachievers.

In my comments in chapter 5 on managing time, I said it is a mistake to treat each piece of paper in your in-box as if it is equal to all others. I might have added that each piece of paper, no matter when handled, should be handled only once. Rereading, reshuffling, and recycling are not only time-wasters, but they spawn confusion and hesitancy.

The same kind of advice can be given about making decisions. That is, there are certain decisions that are far more important than others for you to make *now*. Moreover, since now *is* the time, you should *make* them, you should make them right, and put them behind you. In so doing, you remove any temptation to second-guess yourself. In addition, those dependent on your decisions aren't kept standing on the dime while you labor and stew fruitlessly.

Judicious decisions are the ones hindsight proves to have been right. Whether so-called little decisions or big ones, they demonstrate the exercise of superior judgment.

Superior Judgment

Superior judgment has such a sober sound to it. I suppose this comes from our associating it with rather ponderous pronouncements formulated after learned deliberations by bespectacled, silver-haired men in long black robes. This image, while not representative, is instructive because the point needs to be made that one does not come by superior judgment through birth or privilege. It is earned and learned, over the passage of years, via experience that includes discouragement and heartbreak as much as joy and victory. Accordingly, it is not ordinarily the domain of the young. At any age, however, superior judgment is characteristic of the *alert*.

An animated mind is a fertile garden. And such a seedbed

is where experience can be processed, making best use of the intelligence and fortitude one has at her or his disposal. The highest purpose of a woman or man developing superior judgment is to excel at the endeavor of her or his choosing. Calling the animated mind into the service of excelling in such endeavors is what the late Roger Babson had in mind many years ago when he wrote, "It takes a person who is wide awake to make his dreams come true."

It is the alert, inquiring, processing mind that makes the most of experience; that relates two or more sets of experiences in a learning, growing way, when on the surface they appear to bear no relationship or relevance to each other. Therefore, while the raw mental abilities of analysis and logic are necessary to superior judgment, so is knowing what to make of having been over forty miles of bad road and coming to trust your inner voice. Indeed, the latter two are more likely to produce objectivity and wisdom than the former. My own experience is that my "rational" voice often "lies" to me, whereas my inner or intuitive voice seldom does. Unfortunately, that makes it much harder to listen to. Apparently, I like to be deceived.

Intuition and caring are partners. Intuition tells us what we care about, while what we care about we will struggle long and hard to have treated properly. In other words, when it comes to what we care about, we will leave no option unconsidered, and leave no muscle unmoved in order to see that "it" is made to work. In those cases, it safely can be said that we exercise superior judgment.

Benton & Bowles, a well-known advertising agency, concocted a nifty slogan that opined, "It's not creative unless it sells." The reverse twist here is, "If it works, it was based on superior judgment."

Little Decisions

Superior judgment is necessary to all decisions if they are to be made well, whether they are "little" or "big." Let me first give consideration to the little ones. Little decisions are deceptive. That's because they seemingly don't have as much riding on them. Their ramifications spell neither the summit nor the pits, neither accolades nor pie in the face, neither promotion nor firing.

The people I encounter who habitually cite the refrain to someone or other that "this is a big decision," are women and men who treat *any* decision they have to make as a "big" one. It matters not what the magnitude of the decision is, they have difficulty making it. It sets their knees to knocking, whether they admit it or not.

It is, of course, true that little decisions don't have as high stakes as the big ones when they are taken one at a time. However, when we add up several of them, we usually find that they somehow have *anticipated* what was ahead. And they're seldom unbiased. To impose a human quality on them, they have an ax to grind. In other words, they color what our eyes will be seeing, help shape what issues we will be addressing, and what options we will choose between. Another way of saying all this is that they often set or confirm a hidden agenda! What I'm getting at is that little decisions usually have big implications.

Our inner voice can tell us the implications of the little decisions we choose to make. More than we realize, we're heading in a particular direction, in conformity to some purpose we don't fully understand, and which may or may not be healthful. If it's a healthful purpose or goal, our judgment in reaching decisions will be superior. If the purpose is unhealthful, evasionary or irresponsible in some way, our trail of little decisions is likely to be based on faulty judgment.

If all this seems just a mite too "mystical" for you, let me ask you simply to retrace the steps leading up to your last "big" decision. My guess is that you'll discover the little decisions were in harmony with the big decision whether or not you think the big decision was a good one.

As with all little things, it always is tempting to underplay the importance of little decisions. Little things are always a sign. They are sending a particular message, and that message should not go unheeded. The value of peering into a little decision is that it gives clues on how you can prepare yourself for the big decisions judiciously.

Big Decisions
The executive facing the big decision has the responsibility and opportunity to serve his company and add to his self-esteem in a distinctive way. This is because at the point the decision is reached, he can combine courage and discernment to set (or keep) a company on a solid, appropriate course. Or he can stop it dead in its tracks if it is about to head off in the wrong direction.

The wrong direction emanating from a truly big decision can kill a company right then and there. The corporation may wander around in an undiagnosed delirium for some time—even years—but the fatal dose of poison will have been administered with the truly big decision being made badly. The number of executives who make decisions opportunistically and self-servingly is frightening. It is a tribute, all right, to the resilience of our corporations that they survive many of these decisions. But the real saving grace is the narcissism of these executives. It obscures the fact that most of the decisions they make are not as "big" as they have conjured them up to be in their own minds.

Everett Olson, chairman and chief executive of the Carnation Company in Los Angeles, is a man who strikes me as knowing how to make judicious decisions—little and big. An authoritarian, crusty type, he doesn't suffer fools gladly and he is notoriously closemouthed with the press and financial analysts. As I write this, he is seventy-seven years old and shows no signs of retiring. He has been with Carnation since he graduated from Northwestern University in 1927. He became its president in 1963 and its chief executive in 1971.

Olson's stewardship is criticized in some circles for being overly conservative. The company sits on a cash horde that many observers think is a criminally poor utilization of assets. And while Carnation's main business is in consumer packaged goods—a razzle-dazzle, glamorous field where sophisticated marketing is the order of the day—this company has a reputation for being stodgy and unprogressive.

But the company is very profitable, year after year, and, on average, has been good to its stockholders. Moreover, while some say Olson's age is indicative of a man who creates succession problems for when he ultimately steps down, he has at least three extraordinarily capable top executives in the wings who *admire* him.

Everett Olson has made many judicious little decisions along the way, and they have added up to a successful company that has a good perception of what it is. It is sales-and-production oriented, rather than marketing oriented, and is far more concerned with the bottom line than market share. In this sense, it is an adaptable, more entrepreneurial and "merchant mentality" company than most others of its size ($4-plus billion annual sales) in its business.

In 1981, at an age when a chief executive with a reputation for conservatism is expected to just let the music play out, Everett Olson made a big decision. His plan, now launched, was for Carnation to open a chain of health and nutrition stores. The company has established itself in the consumer's mind as a trustworthy producer of such contemporary products as "Slender" and "Instant Breakfast," and his thought was that such a chain would be a fitting entry in a society increasingly concerned with nutrition, weight control, and physical fitness.

The company has moved with dispatch. Eye-appealing stores are being opened quickly. Consistent with its character, Carnation refuses to divulge its overall plans for this new business, which includes weekly, in-store, medically supervised behavior modification classes for customers who sign up for the weight-control program. However, the company has announced that by the end of 1985 it intends to have well over one hundred such stores in operation in California, Arizona, Colorado, and Texas alone. Further geographic expansion is expected. These stores are company owned; none is franchised. So it is easy to imagine the significant cost to the company of launching this new business.

Obviously, this decision by Everett Olson is not the action of a man playing it safe. However, only hindsight will show if it was judicious. Elements of it are very risky. On the other hand, the decision displays discernment. The concern for health, nutrition, and fitness in our society is not a fad. The new *retail* business for a food producer with a merchant mentality seems like a good fit.

No one knows for sure, but the vibrations I get are that Everett Olson has grasped the responsibility and opportunity to serve his company and add to his self-esteem in a distinctive way.

By so doing, he is a model for much younger executives.*

WRITTEN ACTION PLAN

Suggestions for changing your thought and action to raise your *making judicious decisions* index.

1. Write out ten decisions or prospective decisions that are "floating around in your head" currently and that you are expected to make. Spend a few moments thinking about each and conclude if it is a decision that "is asking to be made *now*." If it is, place a check mark beside it. When you reach the bottom of the list, you will have cleared your mind of

*On September 5, 1984, just as this book was going to press, Carnation management announced that it had agreed to be purchased (subject to stockholder and U.S. Government approval) by the giant Swiss company, Nestlé, which is over three times the size of Carnation. It is not known, therefore, how this alignment will affect Everett Olson's tenure or the new retail business. While it is certainly possible that given his age, Olson may elect to retire at this juncture, all indications point to his remaining firmly in charge of Carnation's business over the intermediate term, and making whatever decisions he deems proper regarding the health and nutrition operation in light of Carnation's new owners and investment priorities.

dissonance and put off until later those decisions that can benefit from "aging." Consequently, you are free to devote your best thinking to the *now* decisions, and to put them behind you in an orderly way.

Repeat this simple priority process whenever you feel decisions are piling up on you.

2. Let your mind roam; jot down as many "little" decisions made within your company or group over the past year that you were privy to and can remember. Jot them down at random, making no attempt at classification.

After you have twenty or so, see if you can discern any pattern from these decisions. See if they are pointing in any particular direction. See if they indicate a company commitment that either confirms or disputes the official top management rhetoric and stated goals. Discern whether or not you think that when added up they are healthful or unhealthful for the company. See if they "anticipated" any big decisions that have been made recently. See if they offer you any lessons about the *kind* of decisions *you* need to make in the future. Determine whether or not you should make decisions that "fit" the pattern—if indeed there is any—or if you should make decisions that may serve as a corrective or counter to them because you think they signal a wrong course.

3. Write out ten "big" decisions you've made on the job over the past five years. Place a check mark beside each one that hindsight has proved to be a right decision.

For each one you have checked, write out in what specific ways that decision, first of all, served your company in a significant way, and second, added to your self-esteem.

Strive to meet these same high standards of performance in all future big decisions you make.

12

Setting Priorities:
Finding Holes, Setting Goals, and
Creating Roles

SETTING PRIORITIES QUIZ

To test your *setting priorities,* please answer the following questions by marking the response item that most closely matches your typical behavior.

1. Do you spend your time and effort looking good rather than being good?
Usually/Often _____ Sometimes/Seldom _____

2. Are you good at finding "holes" in your corporation that need filling?
Usually/Often _____ Sometimes/Seldom _____

3. Are you willing to admit to the existence of "holes" in yourself that need filling?
Usually/Often _____ Sometimes/Seldom _____

4. Are you good at convincing your associates that a "hole" in the company needs filling?
Usually/Often _____ Sometimes/Seldom _____

5. Do your goals turn out to be wishful thinking?
Usually/Often _____ Sometimes/Seldom _____

6. Do you set goals before their time?
Usually/Often _____ Sometimes/Seldom _____

7. Do your goals give birth to the *will to win?*
Usually/Often _____ Sometimes/Seldom _____

8. Do your goals give added meaning to *current* time and space?
Usually/Often _____ Sometimes/Seldom _____

9. Do you eliminate "chores" on the job by *initiating* roles in support of your goals?
Usually/Often _____ Sometimes/Seldom _____

10. Are you a "vacuum cleaner?" Are you a person who takes on tasks nobody else wants?
Usually/Often _____ Sometimes/Seldom _____

MY SETTING PRIORITIES INDEX

To determine your score on the *setting priorities* quiz, check your answers against the correct ones listed in Appendix B.

For each correct answer, give yourself one-half point. Add up the correct answers and mark the rating category that corresponds to your score.

My score _____   _____ Superior   4.5–5.0
(Setting Priorities)   _____ Good   4.0
                            _____ Satisfactory 3.5
                            _____ Fair   3.0
                            _____ Poor   0.0–2.5

SETTING PRIORITIES

One of my favorite achievers in corporate life is an executive vice-president of a large financial services firm. He's known as someone who speaks his mind freely and believes that the shortest distance between two points is a straight line.

Over lunch with him recently, our conversation happened to turn to an executive we both know and think of as indecisive; one who's more concerned with form than substance. Of this executive my friend said simply, "He is a man who would rather look good than be good."

Being an achiever in the executive suite means getting the right things done. And that requires setting priorities and sticking with them. In order to do that, an executive has to answer three questions honestly when facing a potential project. They are: (1) Is this a worthwhile project for the company? (2) Is this the right time to address it? and (3) Is it an appropriate one for *me* to tackle? By answering these questions in the right way, the executive who seeks to be good rather than merely look good, prepares him or herself for a practical three-step process: (1) finding holes, (2) setting goals, and (3) creating roles.

Finding Holes

Finding holes is discovering and giving names to what's missing. A hole can be in oneself or in one's surroundings. The first holes the young executive must find and fill are in education and early exposure. The business world places great value on a college education, so the young would-be executive who hasn't the foresight to embark on one or the fortitude to complete it, is lacking a sense of priority right off the bat. There are exceptions to be sure, but he or she is likely never to achieve distinction in an executive career.

In matters of early exposure, it is the junior executive wise beyond his years who freely acknowledges "what's missing" (nearly everything!) in his inventory of competence. He says to his management that he seeks to *learn* in every way possible from and within the enterprise. The smart young executives today don't boast of their training (including vaunted MBAs from prestigious universities) and what they have to offer their hiring companies. Nor do they overly concern themselves with getting exposure to the corporate top management by insisting on jobs at corporate headquarters. Instead, while they convey self-confidence, they express an eagerness *to be taught* by hands-on involvement in *what makes the business go*. That translates to entry-level exposures in places such as Fargo rather than Beverly Hills; Spartanburg rather than Manhattan; Alpena rather than downtown Chicago. Experience like this fills holes in one's background. Overly specialized experience at corporate headquarters spawns them.

Young or older, any executive increases his or her worth to a corporation by finding holes, articulating their makeup convincingly, and offering a plan for the best way to fill them. For example, a hole may exist in the marketplace, but the priority setter formulates a rudimentary set of ideas on how the corporation can fill the void better and more quickly than the competition. Or he may see that a hole exists in the organization, but can be filled with an imaginative reordering of communication techniques. Departments previously at rivalry with each other are then able to work together. Or a hole may exist in the corporation's making its community aware of its efforts that benefit that community, but the company story has never been told with any verve. The hole-filler convinces the CEO that he knows how such a campaign can be conducted.

In short, holes, or "what's missing," exist in abundance in every corporation. Filling those holes, whatever or wherever they may be, are among a corporation's most important priorities, recognized or not. It is the achiever who finds these holes, dramatizes their existence and conceives ways to fill them.

Setting Goals

While finding holes requires perception, filling them requires setting goals.

Some years ago, I went through a period where I played down the value of goal setting. I thought that goals smothered spontaneity and kept me so captivated with some object or achievement in the future that I bypassed enjoyments and opportunities that were available to me in the present. This is the "stop and smell the roses" argument. I reasoned that goals I set for myself forced me into conforming to some ideal that I never could meet and actually kept me from being *truly* me, *resourceful* me, *participating* me.

I was wrong, of course. Where I went astray was, first of all, that I confused wishful thinking with true goals, and second, I set goals before their time. The first does in fact create dissonance within a person by stifling spontaneity and authenticity. This is because one mistakenly wishes for what he never can have and contrives behavior that lacks zest. This leads to discouragement due to inevitable and repeated failure. The second also robs one of spontaneity and resourcefulness. Certain goals may not in and of themselves be inappropriate for a person, but if they are set too soon, they will not be reached. Yet in the meantime, a person will have kept himself busy with unproductive and unsatisfying activity.

An important question to ask in goal setting, therefore, is: "Is this a goal for today or is it a goal for sometime later?" If it is a goal to be set sometime later, it must be put off. But if it is a goal to be set today, rather than robbing the present of its richness, and smothering one's spontaneity, vigor, and resourcefulness, it gives *added meaning* to current time and space. It does nothing to prevent us from stopping to smell the roses. In fact, it gives us more time to do so.

A true goal set at the right time gives birth to the will to win. And as David V. A. Ambrose has written, "If you have the will to win, you have achieved half your success; if you don't, you have achieved half your failure." True goals pull. They make us focus on what's meaningful and dismiss what is irrelevant. They give direction. Most importantly, they let us know if the behavior we're engaged in at present is purposeful, or a waste of spirit.

Now back to filling holes. It's one thing to find a hole, yet quite another to conclude this is the *time* to attempt to fill it. To repeat, while the goals to be set to fill the hole may be the right ones, the central issue to be settled is whether or not they are goals for now or goals for later.

Creating Roles
What I have in mind as true goals set at the right time are long-range and intermediate ones. As I said, they add richness to the present by giving meaning to current behavior. In other words, the intermediate or long-range goals foster harmonious short-range goals. Such fostering produces an integrated person and unified behavior. In short, it generates fitting roles for getting the right things done.

Having wandered from orthodoxy, and experienced life outside the fold, I returned "home" with greater faith than ever that man is a goal-setting being. We set life goals for ourselves whether we recognize it or not. We sense down deep often enough, I believe, that we end up where we didn't know we were headed, but realize after we arrive that we were guides to our own destiny all along.

We can make this "inevitable" goal-orientation serve us powerfully in setting and sticking with our priorities. We can do so by acknowledging forthrightly to *ourselves* what our true inclinations are. On what do we place value? With what kinds of people do we most enjoy working? In what ways do we most want to be included? In what part of a project's life cycle do we have the most to contribute? Do we assimilate information best by reading or listening? Do we distribute it best by writing or speaking? Do we gravitate toward glamour and bright lights or is brown our favorite color? Do we

like being on the perimeter or at the center? Do we prefer to
see things or feel them? And where do we stand on all these
items on *this* project versus some other? Answers to such
questions are signs of where we're headed that we might not
have realized. Dissonance within us is minimized by acknowledging these leanings, setting long-range and intermediate goals that build on them, and choosing or creating
roles for ourselves that are in support of them. In the last
analysis, this marriage of goals and roles is what constitutes
motivation. Without such motivation, we will not get the
right things done.

The question that begs asking at this point is: *How can
we have this marriage in the executive suite?* It seems we're
always being asked to do things we don't want to do, and
forever are being overlooked for responsibilities and opportunities where we think we can excel.

The answer lies in admitting our passivity and not being
responsible for taking initiative. The organization, like nature, abhors a vacuum. In the absence of initiative, it takes
on a life of its own and generates chores. It is precisely these
"chores" that make up the "things" we find meaningless and
don't want to do. On the other hand, if we become persons
who create roles, we will be the ones who get the plum jobs
for which we often have been overlooked. Moreover, we'll be
the ones who survive management purges that occur during
cutbacks or in the wake of a merger where many positions
get washed away.

Speaking of vacuums as I was, in a meeting today with
a thirty-nine-year-old president of a $3 billion sales com-
pany, I asked what led him to his high position at such a
young age. Among the factors he outlined, he included that
he learned early on to be a "vacuum cleaner." By that he
meant he consistently kept adding jobs to his own that other
executives didn't want to do. These accretions didn't mean
selling out on his inclinations or on long-range goals he had
set for himself, but merely that they provided an opportunity

to take initiative—or create roles—that were in keeping with where he already was headed. In other words, he made them fit his ordering or priorities.

When it comes to our careers, we—and nobody else— are our own tailors. Good tailors set a superior pattern. Then they make sure they stick with it.

WRITTEN ACTION PLAN

Suggestions for changing your thought and action to raise your *setting priorities* index.

1. Think about some tasks that need doing in your company, but that you have avoided for some reason. Write down five of them. Place a check mark beside those that have appeal to you, but also frighten you somehow. If you look inward patiently and objectively, you'll be able to put your finger on what those fears are. By doing so, you'll be able to *name* them. And by naming them, you'll also be finding and naming holes in yourself.

Pick one of those holes and write out a self-development program for filling it that begins today.

Carefully review your written action plan for exercise number 2 in chapter 6, "Growing Stronger by Being Vulnerable."

2. Write a two or three paragraph obituary of yourself (what you would like to have said about you when you're gone). After you have completed that, write out four or five long-range personal goals *implied* in your obituary that you may not have acknowledged previously.

Next, think back as far as you can remember and identify three high points in your life. Write them down. Then, for each one write out, in as much detail as you find helpful, the answers to these questions:

o What did it have that's missing in my life now?

o How can "what's missing" now be recaptured in whole or in part?

o What were my passions/values attached to this high point?

o How can they be recaptured in whole or in part?

3. Keeping in mind any new information you may have gained about yourself from the above exercises, write out five specific job-related goals:

o Make two of them immediate, to be reached within a week.

o Make two of them intermediate, to be reached within a year. One of these should require primarily your individual effort; the other primarily a group effort of which you're a part.

o Make one of them long-range, to be reached in three years.

13

Tenacity:
Nothing Works and Lasts
Unless *You* Do

BEING TENACIOUS QUIZ

To test your *tenacity,* please answer the following questions by marking the response item that most closely matches your typical behavior.

1. Do you believe your associates see you as a person who keeps comin'?
   Usually/Often _____ Sometimes/Seldom _____

2. Do you maintain a sturdy threshold for emotional pain?
   Usually/Often _____ Sometimes/Seldom _____

3. Do you fail to learn and grow from your losses?
   Usually/Often _____ Sometimes/Seldom _____

4. Are you a bad loser?
   Usually/Often _____ Sometimes/Seldom _____

5. Do you believe your "time" is coming?
   Usually/Often _____ Sometimes/Seldom _____

6. Do you have difficulty picking yourself up after a "fair and square" loss in business?
   Usually/Often _____ Sometimes/Seldom _____

7. Are you inclined to feel sorry for yourself?
   Usually/Often _____ Sometimes/Seldom _____

8. Do you get bored easily?
   Usually/Often _____ Sometimes/Seldom _____

9. Will you risk "taking a pounding"?
Usually/Often _____ Sometimes/Seldom _____

10. Are you a "hare" rather than a "tortoise"?
Usually/Often _____ Sometimes/Seldom _____

MY BEING TENACIOUS INDEX

To determine your score on the *being tenacious* quiz, check your answers against the correct ones listed in Appendix B.

For each correct answer, give yourself one-half point. Add up the correct answers and mark the rating category that corresponds to your score.

My score _____   _____ Superior   4.5–5.0
(Being Tenacious Index)   _____ Good   4.0
                            _____ Satisfactory 3.5
                            _____ Fair   3.0
                            _____ Poor   0.0–2.5

BEING TENACIOUS

You might think that I am elevating tenacity well above its merits by considering it as a major component of being judicious. I don't believe I am, and can cite support from some of the most gifted artists and thinkers who have lived—men who might have been tempted merely to fall back on their gifts to get them through—who make a similar connection.

For example, Goethe wrote, "The most important thing in life is to have great aim and to possess the aptitude and the perseverance to attain it." Michaelangelo claimed that "Genius is eternal patience." And in a direct message to those concerned with their careers, Hemingway wrote, "The first and final thing you have to do in this world is to last in it and not be smashed by it, and it is the same way with your work."

Doggedness is the word, isn't it? The image that comes to my mind when I hear tenacity discussed is two dogs vying with each other over final possession of the one bone each has firmly clenched in his teeth. Pulling, straining, and growling—eventually one will tire and give way. Remember, though, that the one which prevails may not necessarily be the stronger of the two.

All by itself, this simple trait of tenacity residing in a woman or man may spell the difference between that woman or man being an achiever or not. If you've going to be an achiever, you've just got to keep comin'.

Tenacity and Attitude

To keep comin', or to "hang in there," requires a particular disposition toward adversity. That disposition is a positive one. This doesn't mean that a person is friendly with adversity and welcomes it warmly into his or her life, but merely that he or she believes it won't last forever; with a little luck, it may even pass soon. In short, the achiever maintains a sturdy threshold for pain. He or she believes that a little stoicism never hurt anybody.

Epictetus, who was born during the reign of Nero, admired his stoic master and philosopher, Musonius Rufus. He proved it by allowing himself to become permanently lamed at the master's hand. According to Celsus, the Roman encyclopedist, "When his master was twisting his leg, Epictetus only smiled and noted calmly, 'You will break it.' and when it was broken, 'I told you so.'"

Epictetus went a bit far in accepting pain in his life, but we have to admit he certainly was good natured about it! We could use a *little* of that nature. Whereas it served him well in facing physical pain that was severe, it can be helpful to us in dealing with emotional pain that for most of us, at least, is not so severe.

We learn from adversity. We learn from our mistakes. We learn from embarrassment. We learn from losses. We learn from criticism. We learn from harsh words and rejection. Moreover, in the process, we grow more gracious, understanding, empathic, forgiving, humble, and wise. We do learn and grow, that is, if we maintain the right attitude toward adversity. That attitude is that *adversity is inevitable, but seldom permanent, and in most cases, given enough time and effort, can be overcome.*

The seasoning, maturing, deepening, dignity, and self-esteem that come to us when we "live well" with grave disappointment over our failure in a matter where we had placed great importance serve to prepare us for greater victories and yet more significant matters in the future. They contribute to our being better victors. Worse than being a bad loser is being a bad winner.

So indeed, living well is the best revenge, except that in this case, it means to learn from defeat with dignity and, if possible, with good humor. This is possible only with the tenacious executive who believes—and in so believing makes it happen—that his or her "time" is coming.

Tenacity and Overcoming

"Nobody wins 'em all," goes the old saying. It is well to remember this cliché when we're doing what we at least think is our best, and things aren't going well. The disciplined salesman knows this when he has labored long and hard with a customer on a potentially big order, only to see it go to a competitor, or, in times of recession, be put off for a year or more. Moreover, in the latter case, he realizes that the sale has to be made all over again. The competition also has another year to get to that customer.

The division manager whose well-conceived plan to build a new plant is turned down by a group executive at head-quarters, also knows this disappointment and must live with it. So does the eager, high-energy, sure-of-himself executive who sees the promotion he thought was his go to someone else.

Sometimes we lose after we have given a project our best shot and it turns out that the timing wasn't right for what we hoped to accomplish. Sometimes we engage in some form of head-to-head confrontation—inside or outside our company—with an able, formidable competitor, and for this time around at least, he or she or that group outperforms us. On these occasions, we're disappointed, but it's "all in the game," as the song says, and it's not that hard to begin again.

However, tenacity is hardest to come by when we suspect or even know there has been some unfairness or foul play in our losing. These are the times when we may feel rage and bitterness and want to lash out at something or somebody. These are also the times when we are inclined to feel sorry for ourselves. The feelings of rage, bitterness, and self-pity are all fully human and perfectly understandable. But they don't help—except to get us through a little time— and that passage of time allows us to renew our spirits and rebuild our strength.

Yet it is exactly at this point, when we're picking our-selves up, that the pain of tenacity is hardest to endure. This is when we begin to look around again to take things on, but it is a critical time when we may be tempted to run from what we care about most because we've just taken a beating at it. This is where the stoicism comes in, and the grimness, and the determination. And though it may not be enjoyable— the resiliency. *Being tenacious is what is called for when we are smart enough to take the long view or confused enough to have lost it.*

Tenacity and Judgment
You will remember that in the last chapter, I said that true goals set at the right time give birth to the will to win. I also said, however, that true long-range and intermediate goals, while set to ensure a better future, give added meaning to the present. Further, I said they foster within us harmonious short-range goals and fitting or appropriate roles for getting things done.

Keeping this simple circle of factors in mind is helpful when we're down and out, when we've been done in by outside forces and influences. Indeed, we know all too well that we are not transported onward and upward, unobstructed and unscathed through some magical pipeline, enroute to our long-range goals. On the contrary, if we have been wise in choosing those goals, prevail, and ultimately reach them, it will be only after we have survived a long series of halting starts, wrong turns, fallbacks, repeated dangers, numerous threats, assorted bruises, wounds, and outright dislocations. We will arrive exhausted but happy. Not until then do we know for sure we have shown good judgment, on balance, and that our tenacity has served us well.

The executives who set true long-range goals and stick with them may not be glamorous and sleek. They may not be at all charismatic in the popular sense. They may strike us as plodders. But in most cases, they end up being the tortoise who passes the hare. True achievement is a long race, and it demands the long view.

There are many hares in corporate life. They are the

excitement seekers. They take great pride in letting the rest of us know that they get bored easily. I imagine this is a thinly veiled attempt to let us know how bright they are. Well, brightness has nothing to do with being bored in this case. Brightness sees opportunity where others miss it. In fact, the hare's boredom and impatience stem from emotional underdevelopment, poor judgment, and unwillingness to risk taking a pounding.

The hares dart; they're quick; they're out up-front fast. But they require constant feedback and instant gratification. They don't endure. They're worn out when the real action starts, and that action almost always takes place later rather than sooner. Not only is their staying power insufficient, but when we look over their early work we usually discover that *quality* is missing there as well. Their solutions to the problems they faced were temporary. Their perceptions were shallow. They were more concerned with form than substance.

Blessed be the tortoises. They would rather be good than look good.

WRITTEN ACTION PLAN

Suggestions for changing your thought and action to raise your *tenacity* index.

1. Think back over your career during the past five to ten years and list what you consider your most "hurtful" failures. Write them down. Review the list to see if any of them can be attributed to your not being persevering enough.

If some fall into this category, place a check mark next to them and note for each the exact point in that project or problem area where the "pain" got too great and you bowed out. If, in fact, you have checked more than one failure, see if there is a pattern to the circumstances or timing in your relenting.

If you do discern such a pattern, be on guard for its repeat on a project you're dealing with now. Determine to grit your teeth and see it through. To do so, even if you lose, will do wonders for your self-esteem. Reclaiming your powers of endurance will make you stronger the next time. Indeed, your "time" will come.

2. Take time to think about all the people you admire and whose histories you know something about. Write down the names of at least ten such people. Place a check mark beside the name of each person who achieved what it is you admire about him or her *without* having to overcome adversity.

For the rest, itemize the main adversity each person had to overcome in order to become distinctive in your mind.

Write down what main adversity *you* must overcome in your present circumstances to achieve the success you seek. Determine to get on with it.

3. Recall some recent performance reviews you received from your boss or bosses. Likewise, consider some straightforward comments you've received about some aspects of your less-than-desirable behavior from friends and others who know you well. Then contemplate your typical actions to see if you allow yourself to "look good rather than be good," to invest in form rather than substance.

If you do, fully acknowledge in what ways by writing them out. Then compare these actions with those of the "tortoises" in your company who would rather be good than look good. Then re-examine your "look good" behavior and ask, "Is this me?" Of course, your answer will be "No." Score one for the authentic you, and savor this "locking in."

14

Cultivating a Sense of Humor: Accepting the Comical in Ourselves

HUMOR QUIZ

To test your *sense of humor,* please answer the following questions by marking the response item that most closely matches your typical behavior.

1. Do you laugh when the joke's on you?
Usually/Often _____ Sometimes/Seldom _____

2. Do you "needle" your associates?
Usually/Often _____ Sometimes/Seldom _____

3. Are your smiles genuine?
Usually/Often _____ Sometimes/Seldom _____

4. Is your laughter nervous laughter?
Usually/Often _____ Sometimes/Seldom _____

5. Do you joke with people to maintain your distance from them?
Usually/Often _____ Sometimes/Seldom _____

6. Do you accept the comical in yourself without hurting your own feelings?
Usually/Often _____ Sometimes/Seldom _____

7. Do you feel *glad* more than mad, sad, or afraid?
Usually/Often _____ Sometimes/Seldom _____

8. Do you impose idealized roles on yourself that you have great difficulty living up to?
Usually/Often _____ Sometimes/Seldom _____

9. Do you act like a grown-up bully?

Usually/Often _____ Sometimes/Seldom _____

10. Do you give thought to the existence of a "wisdom greater than your own"?

Usually/Often _____ Sometimes/Seldom _____

MY HUMOR INDEX

To determine your score on the *humor* quiz, check your answers against the correct ones listed in Appendix B.

For each correct answer, give yourself one-half point. Add up the correct answers and mark the rating category that corresponds to your score.

My score _____   _____ Superior   4.5–5.0
(Humor Index)   _____ Good   4.0
                               _____ Satisfactory   3.5
                               _____ Fair   3.0
                               _____ Poor   0.0–2.5

BEING OF GOOD HUMOR

Often I have wondered why I find most stand-up comedians not funny. Also, I have wondered why we think such comedians generally are unhappy people. I believe the answers to these questions reside in the fact that the form of expression the stand-up comedian has chosen is joke telling. Jokes and jokers most often are lacking in a sense of humor.

Our everyday language shows the negative connotations of the word *joke* in such comments as, "Aha, the joke's on him," or, "Their marriage is a joke." In addition, we usually think the joker himself is a tragic figure. I suspect this has been true since the days of the court jester.

On the other hand, there's some confusion here. The person who is asked, "What's the matter, can't you take a joke?" is said to be lacking a sense of humor. The confusion can be cleared up, however, if we keep in mind that both the joke we tell or play sadistically, and the undue offense we take at a harmless joke, are attempts to exempt ourselves from the not always flattering plight of our own humanness. They are both ways of saying, "That's not me!" These attempts rob us of the legitimate humor that should come to us naturally. It seems certain the stand-up comedian's "art form" has persisted because we sometimes feel the need to make fun of other people. *Yet the comedian's routines bring us only hollow laughter unless we are willing to see ourselves in the joke.*

Joking as Defense
Nowhere will one see joking as defense more in evidence than in the offices and corridors of our corporations. Since joking is humorless unless we see ourselves in the joke, it behooves us executives to notice that we use it to avoid personal vulnerability; to laugh at anybody and everybody but ourselves.

It was irascible Eric Hoffer who pointed out that the

smile is akin to the frightened animal baring his teeth at his enemy. I think he is right in making this connection, though to my mind it does not apply to all smiles, but only to false ones. The false smile and barbed comment directed to an associate constitute a veiled attack that is one of the most common forms of communication in management discourse. We refer to this coupling as "the needle."

Likewise, we joke a great deal when trying to obscure our self-consciousness and fear of failure on the job. Nervous laughter among senior management fills our conference and board rooms on a daily basis. Our sarcasm and laughing along with a colleague at another's expense over some sincerely wrought but unfortunate turn is nothing less than shared relief that a similar fate has not befallen us.

The saddest lesson on false laughter carried to its most harmful extreme is offered in the person who is a hebephrenic schizophrenic. This is a person who laughs at anything and everything, no matter how inappropriately, 365 days a year, but is the most miserable soul on earth.

To be sure, I'm not suggesting that the joking, needling, smiling executive is on the verge of hebephrenia. But what I am saying is that the hebephrenic's use of laughter as the ultimate defense against what he considers the overpowering demands of life shows that this executive's behavior is wrongheaded and based on anything but real humor.

Joking among associates for purposes of defense is a sure sign that executives who are supposed to cooperate, share information, and pool their ignorance for the good of the corporation will be unwilling to do so. It further assures that in all kinds of critical situations, the message sent will not be the message received. Most important, it assures that in fact the bulk of executive action and energy will be devoted to diversionary and evasive tactics designed to cover one's *tuchas* rather than cope with the true business tasks at hand.

Humor as Stress Reducer

Having called attention to the distinction between joking and humor, let me now place greater emphasis on humor itself. *Humor is the ability to accept the comical in ourselves without hurting our own feelings.* It allows us to perceive the more absurd aspects of our behavior with a joyful disposition. It keeps house for warm smiles and mirthful laughter rather than false smiles and frantic laughter. When the going gets rough and we take ourselves, our tasks, and our performance too seriously, it helps us rebound so that we can laugh more easily tomorrow, even if we can't do it today. Given the fact that the events and rigors of living ensure that at various times we will feel glad, mad, sad, or afraid, a sense of humor ensures that we will feel glad more often than we feel mad, sad, or afraid.

Humor reduces the stress in our lives. If we accept the late Dr. Hans Selye's definition of stress as the rate of emotional wear and tear on the body, humor must be viewed as a terribly neglected facet of health care. An overly stressed executive is a wheel out-of-round, or a ship without ballast about to roll and pitch uncontrollably. An overly stressed executive is out of touch with his own humanness; a person who sees himself in an idealized role rather than the human being with foibles that he is.

Humor and Mortality

At first blush, few audiences would appear as little interested in religion as one made up of business executives. While this may be true, in my opinion, the subject of religion should not be skirted because a well-developed sense of humor requires a person's sense of kinship with his God and coming to terms with his own mortality. Some executives may not admit to concern about kinship with a God or a higher "wisdom," but I know of no group more concerned with their mortality.

There are countless statements that have crept into our

speech that indicate how we feel about matters on a deeper level. One of these that I hear frequently from executives is, "Life is too short." The wisdom of these words is that they highlight our sense of mortality in three ways. First, they acknowledge that we're not here for long. Second, they point to the fact that life sometimes can be too demanding *while* we're here. Third, they hint at a *hope* in an afterlife. A further interpretation of the statement is that life is too important to take so seriously. To do so is to throw it away.

Paradoxically, by believing that life is too important to take seriously, one faces his mortality with a sense of humor and lightheartedness. He also expresses his faith that he is true to his birthright, his creation. Taking ourselves too seriously means taking life too seriously. This becomes an overwhelming task for us mortals. It carries responsibilities we can't meet fully and we botch the job. We take on idealized roles for ourselves and grandly strive to fill them. *But we fill them only in our minds!*

Consider the executive who has become the grown-up bully. This is the fellow who never makes a mistake; who is always right; the true believer; the one who insists that everything be done his way because his way is the only way; the one who must have the last word; the only executive who truly cares about the mission of the corporation; the oh, so serious one . . . the humorless one.

In fact, all such beliefs this executive holds about himself are his own phantoms. *He is not perceived by his associates in the way he perceives himself.* His bloated sense of self reveals a shrunken sense of humor and his own inner feelings of helplessness and dreadfully low self-esteem.

Though I have described an executive whose problems are extreme, we can identify with him because to a lesser extent we engage in the same behavior. We may become battle-hardened, but our relationships and health can suffer. What we need is a little softening. We are born with the capacity for humor. It is in our nature. If we lack humor, we are out of touch with our humanness, our mortality, our selves. We are out of touch with our God—that forgiving, forebearing "wisdom" that surrounds us if we will simply acknowledge it.

In the modern age, it has become fashionable to wander about in a halfhearted agnosticism. It clearly is only half-hearted because every poll of the American people shows that over 90 percent of us profess a "belief in God." We sort of believe and we sort of don't. Religion doesn't seem all that real when many of our clergy, synagogues, and churches themselves have lost their identity. Yet we aren't quite willing to let go of our God.

I am reminded of George Bernard Shaw's quip about Christianity. He said the only problem with it is that nobody's ever tried it. His statement is as right today as it was then, and it could apply to just about any religious tradition.

It's time to give up our hanging-bite faith. It's time to 'fess up to believing we are the children of a wisdom that nourishes rather than depletes us. It's time to recognize that the idea of God in our lives is not incompatible with satellites, lasers, petrochemicals, computers, LIFO accounting, smokestacks, and high-tech. It's time to show the good judgment of sharing the responsibilities of life with a redeeming presence and spirit greater than our own. We need that. *All* achievers need that.

Unless we do these things, we'll never be able to see ourselves in the joke.

WRITTEN ACTION PLAN

Suggestions for changing your thought and action to raise your *humor* index.

1. Think about what you laugh at. Think about the *way* you laugh. Think about how often you laugh. Think about how little you laugh. Think about how often you smile. Think about what purpose *your* smile serves. Think about what you're feeling when laughing at someone else. Think about how you feel when you're laughed at. Think about what makes something truly funny and allows you to see yourself without hurting your own feelings.

You should be able to poke fun at yourself and enjoy it. Name three events in the past year (professional or personal) when you played the buffoon; when you took everything too seriously; when you couldn't accept the comical in yourself.

Today, seeing how easy it was for you to act in these ways, will afford you more tolerance when you spot the same signs in others. Accepting the comical in yourself allows you to accept the comical in someone else.

2. Since possessing a sense of humor is a sign of one's acceptance of self and mortality, it offers redeeming benefits to any interpersonal exchange. Consequently, true humor has been a saving grace in many a management situation where anger, hurt, and revenge might be expected to prevail.

Recall two people with whom you have worked whose senses of humor have added greatly to their managerial competence. Write down their names. Beneath each, describe one situation that demonstrates how their accepting the comical in themselves helped win the day for them by winning the respect of their associates.

Write out at least three lessons you learned from their examples that you can apply on your job.

3. In place of needling your peers and subordinates to express an idea or opinion, you have other superior alternatives at your disposal. Write out three of them.

15

Luck:
How You Can Lead
the Charmed Life

BEING LUCKY QUIZ

To test your *luck,* please answer the following questions by marking the response item that most closely matches your typical behavior.

1. Do you blame circumstances for your failures?
Usually/Often _____   Sometimes/Seldom _____

2. Do you see opportunities your associates do not see?
Usually/Often _____   Sometimes/Seldom _____

3. Are you a "hard-luck" executive?
Usually/Often _____   Sometimes/Seldom _____

4. Are you *hesitant* to act on your private judgments?
Usually/Often _____   Sometimes/Seldom _____

5. Do you enviously watch others do what you could have done?
Usually/Often _____   Sometimes/Seldom _____

6. Are you a "Yes, but" executive?
Usually/Often _____   Sometimes/Seldom _____

7. Do you maintain an attitude of expectancy?
Usually/Often _____   Sometimes/Seldom _____

8. Do you put failures behind you quickly?
Usually/Often _____   Sometimes/Seldom _____

9. Do you reject the notion of *can't?*
Usually/Often _____   Sometimes/Seldom _____

10. Do you nurture your associates with your vitality?
Usually/Often _____ Sometimes/Seldom _____

MY BEING LUCKY INDEX

To determine your score on the *being lucky* quiz, check your answers against the correct ones listed in Appendix B.

For each correct answer, give yourself one-half point. Add up the correct answers and mark the rating category that corresponds to your score.

My score _____   _____ Superior   4.5–5.0
(Being Lucky Index)   _____ Good   4.0
                             _____ Satisfactory 3.5
                             _____ Fair   3.0
                             _____ Poor   0.0–2.5

BEING LUCKY

You can bet on it and look like you're gambling, but you won't be. You can count on it absolutely. "What's the *it?*" you ask. Just this: If you make judicious decisions, set the right priorities, are tenacious, and maintain a sense of humor, you're sure to be lucky, and regularly so at that. You'll be said to lead a charmed life.

No one with a jot of intelligence can deny the element of chance that exists in all our lives. However, what deserves the lion's share of our attention is not this element by itself, but how we respond to it when it enters our existence. Further, we need to ponder to what extent we have taken actions and positioned ourselves to foster chance that turns out to be either good *or* bad; the visitation of Dame Fortune or damned misfortune.

It always is tempting to chalk up our failures to fate and circumstance without stopping to think how we might have prompted them. It is common to forge low expectations for ourselves and others so as not to lose face when we or they do not measure up as we believe we or they should. It is understandable to be dispirited and enervated when struck by a thunderbolt that throws our best-laid plans into a shambles. Yet by acting in these ways, we fail to utilize our powers of perception, initiative, and expectancy.

Luck and Perception

The achiever is someone who sees what others are unable or unwilling to see. In addition, she or he insists on being truthful with self and others about the consequences of what comes within her or his field of vision. Such perception and truthfulness enhance her or his ability to seize opportunity and avoid wasted motion, mishap, or outright catastrophe.

What reaps rewards for the seer is *the perception that identifies the purpose of human behavior and the meaning of events.* This combination is readily apparent in the executive who, for example, regularly conceives of new products or services to meet evolving needs, or workable new solutions to meet old problems. Moreover, this executive knows what steps to take with his associates to ensure the outcome he desires.

An executive comes to mind who achieved marked, rapid success early in his career, but later met with abrupt, repeated failure. Now, at age fifty, he flounders, having been through a string of tainted jobs in the past fifteen years where his performance has been marred by mediocrity. This executive came upon hard times primarily because he did not exercise such perception.

He is brilliant and has great facility with numbers. At age thirty-two he became a partner with one of the largest "Big 8" accounting firms. He did so at a time when partners ordinarily weren't named until their mid- or late-thirties. He clearly was fast-track. In addition, he has great charm and is thought of as a "nice guy."

The same ability and ambition that won him partnership at thirty-two also led him to accept a corporate position as financial vice-president. In this, too, he pioneered a bit, because in the late 1960s, it was almost unheard of for anyone who had earned the distinction and monetary rewards entailed in Big 8 partnership to forsake it for other endeavors.

It was when he joined his first corporation that his career problems began. While well-known, the corporation was on shaky financial ground. This pleased him, however, because the job offered what he called a high-risk, high-reward opportunity. But although he was aware of the limited financial resources of this firm—something that many companies overcome with an imaginative turnaround effort—he overrated the quality of its top management. He completely misread their ability to stage a comeback. Such a career misstep can be made by anyone, of course, but this man has repeated the same error five times since leaving the accounting firm.

Not only has this executive been a poor counselor to himself, but he has been so to others. His steadily declining accomplishments have resulted from his offering faulty perception and unfounded support to his associates and superiors on the marketing and investment decisions they faced together. His advice has been notably bad on matters where he was supposed to be knowledgeable and trustworthy.

This man's avoidance of perception was expressed in his wishful thinking. He denied what was before his eyes and loathed being a receiver or bearer of bad news. This meant that on those occasions where it was critical for him to call 'em as he saw 'em, he found it more comfortable to "support" his bosses in the errors of their ways rather than be a strong dissenter to their misguided moves.

Hooking up with one weak company after another (habitual wishful thinking in lieu of perception) he plunged into a defeatist cycle by indulging his penchant for polishing brass on sinking ships. As one company after another came crashing down—partially due to his refusal to admit to sick scenarios and blow the whistle—his ready refrain (with a dozen variations) was, "I never anticipated the difficulty we were going to have with . . ."

This "hard-luck" executive, and legions like him, create their own luck. Tragically for them, and those who depend on them, most of it is bad.

Hesitancy and Judgment

The foregoing example of the hard-luck executive shows that although the power of perception was available to him, he refused to use it. To repeat, he found it more comforting (though ultimately disastrous) to engage in denial and wishful thinking. This meant, therefore, that his shortcoming was not analytical or logical, but behavioral.

A similar criticism can be aimed at executives who don't lack for good judgment, but are hesitant to act on that judgment. In their case as well, their shortcoming is behavioral.

They set needless limits on what they are able to achieve. They miss opportunities to create their own good luck. They stand by and watch others do what they know they should have, but didn't for fear of failing at it.

Herodotus said, "All men's gains are the fruit of venturing." This wise man of old never would counsel that we undertake ventures that have not been thought out carefully, but simply that good fortune cannot come to the person who refuses to risk testing his judgments with his own initiatives. The exercise of good judgment is doing the right thing in the right way. If an executive regularly combines doing the right thing in the right way with doing so at the right *time*, he or she often will be called lucky. And while the overly eager person can ruin a venture by taking it on too soon, it is the achiever who concentrates on overcoming the hesitancy that would let pass the right time for taking initiative.

"Yes, but" is a killer. It is an expression of lowered expectations for our performance on a project. When we say "Yes, but" we're saying "No" without clarity. We're saying we can't do it. We're saying we *won't* do it. We're saying we're afraid to try it. We're saying that to try and fail borders on a fate worse than death. We're saying we don't trust our judgments.

Confidence in our judgment grows in leaps and bounds when we say "No" plainly because we consider a possible venture unsound, or "Yes, by God" and run with it because we believe in it. It is by taking initiative aggressively that we make things happen and, by making them happen, are more willing to repeat the process next time around. Even when our initiatives don't pan out as well as we would like, neither do our catastrophic fantasies materialize. It is the aggressive ball club that makes its breaks by being disconcerting to the opposition. Likewise, it is the achiever who builds good luck by pressing hard with his judgments.

Expectancy and the Charmed Life

When combined with desire, expectancy produces hope. Hope makes purposeful action possible. Relevant to the latter is a statement from Washington Irving, one of our most perceptive early American writers. He wrote, "Great minds have purposes; others have wishes." His insight leads to the realization that without expectancy, we lack purpose.

What I find particularly admirable in achievers is their attitude of expectancy. This shows itself most forcefully in the way they minimize their losses and celebrate their victories. People who work closely with achievers cannot help but notice that they are not subject to "bereavements" from those achievers. That is, the achiever does not grieve over his failures or bemoan what might have been.

On the other hand, the achiever enjoys his successes and accomplishments to the fullest and draws his associates into the celebration. Moreover, he looks around the corner in anticipation of additional good things that await him. All he has to do, he believes, is show a little determination to get them.

One very simple reason we think of some achievers as leading charmed lives is that we hear about their victories, while they quickly put their failures behind them with little mourning or fanfare. This does not mean, however, that the accomplished executive denies those failures, or refuses to learn from them. It is only that he chooses to get on with something constructive when they occur.

Entrepreneurs are among the best examples of achievement and of maintaining an attitude of expectancy. These people who invest gargantuan amounts of time and energy—and often risk their life savings—to start a business, seldom contemplate failure. Virtually every moment they devote to their work is given over to mobilizing themselves and their people to seize opportunities that they see abounding all around them.

Such expectancy brings its rewards. Entrepreneurs who

succeed end up far wealthier than even the chief executives of many of our largest publicly held corporations. Moreover, by dint of their faith, sweat, and imagination, they have built something from scratch, and can take pride in the success they brought about *against great odds*.

While successful entrepreneurs serve as good examples of what expectancy can generate in personal and group performance, *all* executives who nurture this attitude will find themselves leading charmed lives. This is because they increasingly become people who embrace *life!* They become people who reject the notion of *can't;* people of poise and conviction. As a result of this commanding presence, they are able to open more doors than others, strike better deals, and attract more energetic, resourceful people to stand beside them. They set higher standards and get their people to meet them. They win confidence. They are not a negative, impairing influence on their associates, but nurture them with their own vitality.

The charmed life is the expectant life, and living the expectant life is an act of good judgment.

WRITTEN ACTION PLAN

Suggestions for changing your thought and action to raise your *being lucky* index.

1. Write down the names of five "hard-luck" executives you have known. For each, record one way that her or his behavior assured "bad luck" and failure. For example, you might write, "George's habitual 'yes, but' decisions to our recommendations were designed to absolve himself of responsibility with the big boss. We weren't going to bite at that bait, so we just let those initiatives fizzle out. As a result, he never got more than halfhearted efforts from us."

For other examples, recall the story of the hard-luck financial executive I told.

Review these five sets of behavior to make sure none of them is characteristic of you. If any is, strike it from your inventory immediately, because ultimately it will defeat you.

2. Unrealistically high expectations that never can be met are dispiriting and self-defeating. However, low expectations also are self-defeating and a face-saving way of letting ourselves off the hook. If we won't ask much of ourselves, we won't have to deliver much.

List three projects in which you're engaged where you have forged low expectations for yourself. Under each, describe how these low standards compromise your abilities and keep you from experiencing your strength.

For all three, raise the bar and ready yourself for a higher leap. Write down your revised expectations.

3. Compile a list of fifteen people with whom you work and whose output is important to your effectiveness. Some of these people are *nurturing*. That is, they brighten and lighten whatever they touch. They're encouragers and contributors. They have much to give. Some will be *impairing*. That is, they darken and burden whatever they touch. They're discouragers and withholders. They take more than they give.

Go down your list and place either an *N* (for nurturing) or an *I* (for impairing) beside each name. Notice which type predominates on the list. The lesson is obvious: shed as many impairers as possible from your joint efforts and avoid them like the plague in the future.

Now skip a space and add your name to the bottom of the list. In your opinion, what letter would most nurturers on your list place beside your name? Place that letter there yourself and circle it.

Are you carrying your weight with these nurturers?
Yes _____ No _____ (check one)

MY JUDGMENT INDEX

To determine your *judgment index,* add up your scores from the quizzes listed below. Then mark the rating category that corresponds to your score.

Making Judicious Decisions   _____

Setting Priorities   _____

Tenacity   _____

Sense of Humor   _____

Being Lucky   _____

My Judgment Index   _____

_____ Superior   22.5–25.0

_____ Good   20.0–22.0

_____ Satisfactory 17.5–19.5

_____ Fair   15.0–17.0

_____ Poor   0.0–14.5

IV

RESOURCEFUL

Mere diligence can never do in a dozen years what talent does in a day; yet at the same time, talent without diligence keeps squandering its inheritance and soon goes bankrupt.

SYDNEY J. HARRIS

A N INCOMPREHENSIBLE amount of human time and effort has gone into the thinking, writing, and discussion of creativity. It is a subject that fascinates us perhaps more than any other. We're drawn toward those executives we consider creative, and, we must admit, we're more than just a bit envious of them, too. There seems to be no limit to what they are able to produce that the rest of us can enjoy or make use of in some way.

Yet a good part of our envy is unnecessary because we misunderstand what "creativity" is. The word itself gets in the way. For the rarest of the rare, as with a Beethoven, creativity has a special meaning. But for everyone else, including the denizens of the executive suite, creativity is nothing more or less than a person's making full use of his or her resources. Those resources exist *within* the person and also *surround* him or her.

This section is the part of the book that deals with creativity on the job. But the subject is, as it should be, *resourcefulness*. What goes into the making of a resourceful executive is: (1) the commitment to deliver the goods; (2) learning to think beyond the obvious; (3) refining one's gifts; (4) training oneself to be a facilitator; and (5) the discipline to exercise vision.

Continue your *achiever development program* by conducting an assessment of your commitment to "deliver the goods."

16

The Ultimate Commitment: Delivering the Goods

DELIVERING THE GOODS QUIZ

To test your *delivering the goods,* please answer the following questions by marking the response item that most closely matches your typical behavior. Remember, you have everything to gain by being objective in your replies. No one but you will see the results.

1. Do you succeed in conveying a sense of concern for details to your subordinates?
Usually/Often _____   Sometimes/Seldom _____

2. Do you ponder the *unarticulated* goals of your corporation?
Usually/Often _____   Sometimes/Seldom _____

3. Do you set your own performance goals without regard for those unarticulated goals?
Usually/Often _____   Sometimes/Seldom _____

4. Do you neglect looking into your corporation's rhetoric for symbols, or an overall *message,* of what it is committed to?
Usually/Often _____   Sometimes/Seldom _____

5. Do you feel you have a good sense of what your associates want from you in your work?
Usually/Often _____   Sometimes/Seldom _____

6. Do you draw praise from your peers and superiors for your work?
Usually/Often _____   Sometimes/Seldom _____

154

7. Do you visualize the persons you serve *within* your corporations as *customers* to be pleased?
Usually/Often _____   Sometimes/Seldom _____

8. Do you serve "systems" more than people?
Usually/Often _____   Sometimes/Seldom _____

9. Are you late to meetings and appointments?
Usually/Often _____   Sometimes/Seldom _____

10. Do you count deadlines you have agreed to as a trust?
Usually/Often _____   Sometimes/Seldom _____

MY DELIVERING THE GOODS INDEX

To determine your score on the *delivering the goods* quiz, check your answers against the correct ones listed in Appendix B.

For each correct answer, give yourself one-half point. Add up the correct answers and mark the rating category that corresponds to your score.

My score _____   _____ Superior   4.5–5.0
(Delivering the Goods   _____ Good   4.0
Index)   _____ Satisfactory 3.5
                            _____ Fair   3.0
                            _____ Poor   0.0–2.5

DELIVERING THE GOODS

We all know that *delivering the goods* is a figure of speech that refers to following through on a commitment. Further, we realize that following through on a commitment is a sure sign that the deliverer is acting on his or her talents rather than turning in an ordinary or mediocre performance.

One exemplary element in avoiding mediocre performance can be seen in a lesson Jesus taught his disciples that is as relevant today as ever. He said that the person who is not faithful in the little things also will not prove faithful in the bigger things. His point was not that the little things in life and work are more important in themselves, but that unless a person cares for them it is unlikely he will be able to deliver on the larger challenges he will face. He is wise who never loses sight of the fact that faithfulness to the small matters serves as a foundation for mastery in the large ones.

It may seem like a contradiction to insist that attention to the little things is an integral part of the big picture. After all, isn't it the able executive who has learned to do first things first, and second things hardly ever? The answer to this question is, of course, an automatic "Yes." But the confusion comes from thinking that the little matters—however they get defined in a specific instance—are not among the first things. Concern for detail, for example, may well be delegated, but it always should be clear that the achieving superior keeps an eagle eye out for attentiveness in this area. Such attention to detail is indicative of a superior who has the big picture on *all* that is required to fulfill our purposes, with quality performance, in a timely fashion.

Sense of Purpose

It is impossible for the executive committed to mastery to deliver the goods consistently without articulating his or her own sense of purpose. That sense of purpose comes into focus by asking and answering two questions: (1) What is my company here for? and (2) What am I here for? Both questions are more difficult to answer than is apparent.

I believe that we talk most doggedly about what we are least willing or able to do. As a result, our rhetoric far outstrips our performance. This is no less true of corporations than individuals. While I also believe it is paramount that corporations and individuals set goals, experience and research show that a preponderance of such goals are never met, giving rise to the suspicion that they are not real goals. Real goals—goals "from the stomach"—often are not articulated but *are* met. These are goals that are imbedded in the value system of a corporation that constitutes a better part of what we're now calling *corporate culture.*

Since most corporations are not skilled in articulating their real goals—in other words, their purpose—the achiever is careful to devote time and effort to perceiving what that purpose is, and sets his performance goals accordingly. After all, even profit itself is not automatically a corporation's main goal. Most corporations regularly make decisions and take actions that compromise the maximization of profit. I am not saying this is wrong, but merely that the canny executive acknowledges this fact as he charts his own course.

Another example can be seen in the large number of corporate top managements who profess dedication to long-range planning. Yet when their actions are scrutinized, many will have departed from their plans. Further, just as many often will place a failed top executive, or an executive coasting to retirement, in charge of the planning function. A wise, young, aspiring executive obviously will look for a detour around the planning department in his coveted climb up the ladder in such companies.

It follows, then, that delivering the goods is defined differently in each corporation. Moreover, the executive committed to such delivery has to articulate a sense of purpose in harmony with the corporate definition. This is not cynical in the least. Virtually all corporations provide a wide berth for all but the most pure in thought or hopelessly naive to give what they have in true talent and enlightened self-interest.

An executive who spends the necessary time exploring and discerning his corporation's purpose will find himself in a position to develop his most worthy subordinates and out-perform his peers. Because of this, he also will please his superiors. They will think of him as a self-starter who is marked by good judgment. And while he doesn't overinvest in official corporate rhetoric, he will not dismiss it, but rec-ognize it as some sort of *symbol* of what the corporation cares about deep down. Because he is aware of the gap between many spoken goals and actual ones, he also is able to be an instrument to help the corporation bring the two into har-mony.

Quality Goods

Delivering the goods means giving a quality performance. Surely the root of *goods* has much to do with someone re-ceiving something favorable. It is the person on the receiving end who renders the final verdict on the quality of what is served up. He or she determines what is *good.*

Service given in the right place is what assures the right-ful receiver of quality performance. Service is often sacrificed because individuals and corporations allow themselves to get caught in the trap of serving their "systems" rather than making their systems serve the right receivers. By this I mean that often we serve our own convenience, or see to it that "proper procedures" are followed that simplify *our* efforts. In the interim, the party who rightfully needs and deserves our utmost attention is given short shrift or delayed.

For example, a corporation may consolidate its various divisional sales forces into one centralized sales force where each sales person is now expected to be able to sell *all* the company's products. Such a sales force will be smaller and easier to manage, and, therefore, more cost-efficient (at least on the surface). But the sales persons now are required to be knowledgeable and care about a host of more products. Many of them will not measure up on this score, however, and consequently many customers will be less well served. Corporate "systems" and "efficiencies" are cared for, but the all-important customer is not.

The question that needs asking by any person who wants to provide real service is: "Am I participating in the main event or merely a sideshow?" This question is equally pertinent whether it concerns service owed to the ultimate customer, or someone within the corporation who is a link on the way to satisfying that customer—the entity that is the corporation's reason for being.

An overwhelming amount of rhetoric is given to service in our corporations and, given my convictions on rhetoric, you know why I find this disturbing. Service has become a cliché, much like the perfunctory statements in many annual reports to the effect that "our people are our most important asset."

The achiever makes sure that service is not a cliché. He realizes his function is not to make systems serve him, but his receivers. If they don't serve his receivers, he works to win approval for abandoning or circumventing them in favor of actions that do. Failing that, he hangs tough until future events reveal that his way may be better than what has been laid down by his bosses.

It is helpful to think of our receivers (whomever they may be) as our customers, and the definition of quality becomes clear when these "customers" experience satisfaction with what they receive. Being committed to doing all that we can to create such satisfaction is the true marketing attitude. Wherever companies can instill this attitude—the aim to please—among all their employees as well as to end-users, they create an atmosphere where quality performance prevails and people take pride in delivering on their commitments.

On Time

No matter how committed we are to delivering quality goods, our performance is tarnished (if not spoiled) if we are tardy in meeting our obligations. In fact, it is taken for granted that among accomplished executives delivering the goods means "the goods" arrive on schedule. It is sad but true that many executives fail to grasp the brass ring for no other reason than they have a poorly developed sense of time and timeliness.

I always am surprised at the number of executives who have little comprehension of how much time their projects will take. Whether a project will stretch out over an hour, a day, or several months, they grossly misjudge what time will be demanded of them and their speed at work. The signs of such executives are tardiness for appointments, delay in returning phone calls, and habitual claims of unforseen circumstances slowing them down in their efforts.

The achiever treats a deadline he has agreed to as *sacred*. He hates to be late for an appointment, and an unreturned phone call—except to a pest—gnaws at his innards. Odd as it may seem, in many companies these fundamental niceties make him a hot knife through butter. They are scarce.

While meeting deadlines is a mark of achievers, they are careful not to count on it automatically from others. Some of those on whom one depends will offer rosy forecasts on the timely completion of their tasks. Skepticism is appropriate because the rhetoric on timing may be even more bogus than the rhetoric on corporate goals. Though it may be sincere, it may not be realistic.

The balance to be struck in facing one's timing commitments is to maintain control over one's *own* work habits while agreeing to deadlines (for superiors) that take into account the poor time concepts of those on whom we may have to depend. Where we have leverage—as with subordinates—we can make more things happen. But where getting what we need is based on persuasion and winning cooperation, we are stuck with our best guesses on the time elapsing before our commitments can be brought to fruition.

The hard-nosed prognosticating of the performance of others, combined with the collaborative effort to secure desired results, is the kind of pressure and ambiguity the modern executive who follows through on his or her commitments must be willing to bear. While the whip is as outmoded and ineffective as grandma's homegrown remedy, anything less than a full-court press to meet deadlines will produce a spiritless, mediocre outcome for the receiver who is counting on us to deliver the goods.

WRITTEN ACTION PLAN

Suggestions for changing your thought and action to raise your *delivering the goods* index.

1. Write out ten shibboleths (pet phrases) of your corporation's "in-house" standard rhetoric. Force yourself to look beyond their literal content for clues to discover or confirm your corporation's sense of purpose. Write down at least three overall "messages" conveyed by these shibboleths that reveal what your corporation is about.

List three personal goals of yours that deserve scrutiny and possible revision because they *may* be in opposition to your corporation's purpose as you understand it. Continue to think about these goals over the next month before reaching any hard conclusions.

2. List at least two "systems" you serve—or make serve you—that do not therefore properly serve your rightful receivers. Discuss these systems with relevant associates to determine ways to alter the systems to serve such receivers. Help make these modifications quickly.

Think about all your current corporate projects and in-volvements. List any that you consider sideshows rather than main events. Shed them at the earliest possible moment.

3. Recount your daily "timeliness performance" over the past week:

- ○ Did you return all telephone calls within twenty-four hours?

- ○ Were you on time to all meetings and appointments?

- ○ Did you meet all deadlines?

Your answer to all questions should be a hard "Yes."

17

The Executive's
Hidden Challenge:
Thinking Beyond the Obvious

THINKING BEYOND THE OBVIOUS QUIZ

To test your *thinking beyond the obvious,* please answer the following questions by marking the response item that most closely matches your typical behavior.

1. Do you rush to apply the latest advances in your field to your work?
   Usually/Often _____   Sometimes/Seldom _____

2. Are you committed to applying the obvious, the routine, the mundane?
   Usually/Often _____   Sometimes/Seldom _____

3. Do you believe that what most of your associates think of as obvious requires no further thought from you?
   Usually/Often _____   Sometimes/Seldom _____

4. Do you give thought to the ways your company *acts* that you and your associates do not understand?
   Usually/Often _____   Sometimes/Seldom _____

5. Do you believe "form follows function"?
   Usually/Often _____   Sometimes/Seldom _____

6. Do you give thought to the ways your corporation's forms are not compatible with its functions?
   Usually/Often _____   Sometimes/Seldom _____

7. Do you rely on "cause/effect" thinking on complex issues; that the "sum of the parts equals the whole"?
Usually/Often _____   Sometimes/Seldom _____

8. Do you rely on "the parts anticipate the whole" thinking on complex issues?
Usually/Often _____   Sometimes/Seldom _____

9. In group discussions with your subordinates, do you actively attempt to "anticipate the whole" for the department you manage?
Usually/Often _____   Sometimes/Seldom _____

10. Do you allow the department you manage to *drift* by not squarely facing its tradeoffs?
Usually/Often _____   Sometimes/Seldom _____

MY THINKING BEYOND THE OBVIOUS INDEX

To determine your score on the *thinking beyond the obvious* quiz, check your answers against the correct ones listed in Appendix B.

For each correct answer, give yourself one-half point. Add up the correct answers and mark the rating category that corresponds to your score.

My score _____	_____ Superior	4.5–5.0
(Thinking Beyond the	_____ Good	4.0
Obvious Index)	_____ Satisfactory	3.5
	_____ Fair	3.0
	_____ Poor	0.0–2.5

THINKING BEYOND THE OBVIOUS

For a long time I have believed that one of the big differences between the nonachiever and the achiever is that the latter has mastered the art of applying the obvious. Rather than making use of exotic ideas with sophisticated applications, it is distinctive, consistent performance in seemingly mundane areas that spells success in almost any undertaking. To my mind, this explains why in most Super Bowl games, a "plodding" Green Bay Packers or Pittsburgh Steelers will come out on top of a razzle-dazzle Dallas Cowboys.

Further evidence for my convictions was provided by Peter Drucker in a December, 1982 interview with *Psychology Today*. Drucker says that he has become fairly abrasive in his consulting relationships with his corporate clients. He says that dropping hints doesn't work. He mentions that on many occasions he will spend a day with a client, and then be scolded by that client that he hadn't told him and his associates to do anything they didn't already know. He relishes these times and says his standard reply to their indictment is one of his own: "Then why in hell haven't you done it?" (Notice that Drucker's question is *not* a question. See chapter 2 on listening.)

While Drucker's "question" underscores that it is indeed the application of the obvious that leads to success, it also got me to wondering why doing the obvious is so difficult, and, therefore, relatively rare. The conclusion I've reached is that often the "obvious" is not what it seems. As a result, it is misunderstood and much executive action is misdirected.

Cause and Effect

In short, the obvious isn't so obvious. For example, when we encounter problems, it is obvious we should look for causes. When we seek to understand successes so that we can repeat them, we should look for causes. When we want to know why an associate behaves in a particular way in a situation, we should look for causes. When we want to learn why our competitors are beating us in the market, we should look for causes. When we want to understand our failures at consummating successful acquisitions, we should look for causes. When we seek to comprehend the stultifying "bureaucracy" that overcomes our companies after they have grown rapidly, we should look for causes. All this is indicated. It cannot be argued. All this is obvious. Right?

Wrong! For centuries before any of us were born, our world has taken for granted that by understanding causes we can solve virtually any problem or achieve any effect we desire. In theory this is true, but the knotty issue presented by increased understanding and experience in life all around us is that "causes" often are elusive. We routinely find that when we take action to eliminate the causes we have defined as culprits, our problems do not go away. Or when we insist on certain ingredients being present in our actions because we think they cause success, we discover that for some reason, success is not repeated.

We have believed that by understanding parts, we can know the whole. Thus we can make the whole what we want. "The parts *cause* the whole" is the underpinning of our thought process. The whole is the *effect* of the parts. Poverty and all that goes with it cause crime; high salaries cause a high-morale executive team; an abrasive CEO causes poor morale; the finest product will cause the most success in the marketplace. Such bromides are sure to lead us astray.

As proof that the "causes" aren't causes, let us reverse the bromides. Their opposites are equally arguable: crime and all that goes with it causes poverty; a high-morale executive team causes high salaries; poor morale causes an abrasive CEO; success in the marketplace causes the finest products. It is clear that what we typically think of as both "causes" and "effects" are expressions of a yet more encompassing whole.

What we have thought of as causes are most often *effects*. This is not obvious, but should be. They are parts that are not causes, but *outcomes*. They result from anticipation and expectation. This expectation is an underground "wisdom." Ordinarily, it is not *articulated*. Typically, it is not even *acknowledged* and for the most part, it is not *sensed* by the actors in the drama of our everyday lives, however rudimentary that drama may be.

The obvious message we miss is that *the parts emerge in anticipation of the whole*. In other words, in our individual and corporate lives, we select the bits and pieces of our thought and action to accommodate or enhance our place in what we anticipate to be the whole or end. There is a "system" at work, but we may not be at all aware of it.

Function

It was Louis Sullivan, the father of the skyscraper, who wrote in 1896 that "form ever follows function." A brilliant architect, he was of course describing the physical realm, but his words are just as true of the behavioral realm. Function is end; function is goal; function is purpose; function gives rise to form. Form is system.

System serves function; system is created in response to function. Form is parts; parts exist in anticipation of function. Function is whole; whole is goal. Goals can be acknowledged or unacknowledged. They can be healthful or nonhealthful, appropriate or inappropriate, for individuals and corporations alike.

Most of the time we executives concern ourselves with form, addressing its conformity or lack of it with our rhetorical goals. We tend to do this without facing the fact that when form is not in conformity to our rhetorical goals, it is very likely to be operating efficiently in conformity to our unacknowledged goals. Far more than we realize, we behave in harmony to our pulls rather than our pushes. Our goals— our purposes—whether we are truly aware of them or not—

have a far greater impact on us. And rather than knowing the whole through its parts, we are more likely to understand the parts by knowing the whole. All this is not obvious until we think it through. Then it is.

There are manifest and latent forms of behavior. Normally, we concern ourselves with the manifest, but would be wise to direct more of our attention to the latent ones.

Manifest forms of behavior are those that are given rhetorical consensus and sanction. They are actions based on the generally believed reasons for which a plant is built, a division is created, or the president elects to centralize management. Latent forms of behavior are the underlying and usually unwitting actions taken that show (for the perceptive) *how* things truly are. While they answer such questions of how, the manifest answer *why* things *should* be, even though they're not. Manifest forms are up front and expressed in rhetoric; latent forms are down below and remain silent. Manifest forms are the facade; latent forms are the substance. Our corporations have values and a "wisdom" all their own. These reside in their latent forms of behavior. Anyone claiming to understand corporate culture without taking into account manifest and latent forms of behavior is making a false claim.

On one level, the new president reorganizing the company serves the goal of making it more efficient while cutting costs. On a deeper level, the new president may be establishing his or her authority while portraying him or herself as a person of action.

The manifest reason for conventions and trade shows is to keep industry members up-to-date on trends and developments. The latent reason may be to provide a vehicle for keeping up with industry contacts when members need to change jobs.

The manifest reason for the annual performance appraisal is to provide for an objective evaluation of executive achievement and a basis for future training. The latent reason is to encourage a political climate in which subordinates curry favor with their bosses because they know there is no way such appraisals can be objective.

We may want to *believe* in our corporate manifest (obvious) forms, but more than we usually admit, we are governed by the latent ones.

Tradeoffs

The late Vince Lombardi often was criticized for saying that winning was not the most important thing, but "the *only* thing." I think his critics misunderstood him. He knew what his tradeoffs were. He knew he had certain mutually exclusive choices to make and to convey to his players. He was clear on the team's function—giving its very best—and WINNING IS THE ONLY THING was a rallying cry that made clear to the players what forms were required to serve that function.

The "corporate culture" of the Green Bay Packers in Lombardi's day was one where manifest and latent forms were the same. This absence of dissonance led to their unrivaled effectiveness. So the "obvious" execution for which Lombardi and his Packers were famous was based on the nonobvious realization of what their true goals were. Goals are so easy to spit out. However, it takes a great deal of reflection and perception to know what goals are truly appropriate for an organization. Winning itself isn't a function unless it is considered as a yet larger whole in some "final" eschatological sense. The belief in Heaven is an example of this. However, that does not concern us here. The same can be said for a high return on assets. Therefore, a high return should—as with winning—be viewed as a *measurement*.

Without realizing it, companies routinely invite latent forms to sabotage manifest ones when they come to forks in the road and think they can go both ways. The word *tradeoff* became a more predominant part of business vocabulary starting in the early seventies. We used the word, but didn't pay attention to what it meant. Now we're beginning to. It signifies a fork in the road. *I consider this concept one of the most important considerations that any management claiming to do strategic thinking and planning can impose upon itself.* This is one way a corporation ensures being honest with itself. For example, a company that claims it can grow in annual volume from $400 million to $4 billion without becoming more bureaucratic and less entrepreneurial is deceiving itself. A tradeoff for size is the necessity for additional controls and an increase in formal communication accompanied by slower movement and decision making. This is as incontrovertible as the leopard's inability to change his spots.

While some companies are more bureaucratic than others of the same size, *all* $4 billion companies are more bureaucratic than all $400 million companies. The error of a corporation's ways is not that it becomes more bureaucratic as it grows, but that it engages in rhetorical wishful thinking and wasted motion. Successful growth companies *manage* bureaucracy by reducing it wherever possible, but they do not deny its existence and expect their people to do the same. In this critical organizational issue they face their tradeoffs as they must in many others as well. This is obvious, yet it obviously isn't.

WRITTEN ACTION PLAN

Suggestions for changing your thought and action to raise your *thinking beyond the obvious* index.

1. Write out three persistent problems you have been involved with during the past two years; problems you thought you had solved, but turned out *not* to be solved. Examine your "solutions" to these problems to see if they were based on cause/effect thinking. Examine them further to see if what you thought were causes were indeed "effects."

Now explore the possibility that these "effects" were

outcomes of anticipating some whole you have not yet en-
visioned. Consider how the "problem" is a response to a *pull*
rather than a *push*.

2. Think carefully about how your company is structured
and how it operates. Think about what gets done and how.
Write out three "forms" you've observed that strike you as
sturdy and entrenched, yet don't seem to jibe with your corporation's rhetorical goals. Keeping in mind that "form ever
follows function," let your mind play to enquire what function (end, goal, purpose, whole) each of these forms (practices, structures) might be serving of which you and your
associates are not aware. Write down what you sense.

For example, your thinking might run like this: "Our
chairman constantly hammers away at wanting to make acquisitions and develop new products. I'm glad for that because we're basically a one-product company. It's a whale
of a product—the best in the business—and we dominate
the market. We're much more profitable than our closest
three competitors put together. Yet how long can this goose
be counted on to lay the golden eggs? Y'know, I've been to
Harvard! I've heard Ted Leavitt on how you have to even
plot the obsolescence of your product. Yep, the CEO's right
to keep us committed to acquisitions and new products. It's
weird, though. I've been here twelve years and have been
through gobs of acquisition studies and lots of new product
research. The fact is, we've not made even one tiny acquisition or brought even one new product to market. Thank
God we're so profitable! Huh . . . maybe despite the chairman's words, and despite the fact that he might believe deeply
he is sincere, maybe down in the recesses somewhere he
really believes we need a new product like we need a hole
in the head. Or maybe, since he's near retirement, he doesn't
want to rock the boat or maybe . . . hey, this could be it
. . . yeah . . . I just saw it in a Mark Twain quotation in the
airline magazine flying back yesterday from Baltimore. Twain

said, 'Put all your eggs in one basket, and watch the basket!'
Oh boy, that's it. That fits. That's what the chairman *really*
believes! I don't know if he's right but sure as shootin' that's
what he believes. Yeah, when I think of his actions rather
than his words, the pieces all come together."

3. Label and write down at least one fork in the road (tradeoff) that the group you manage soon will be facing. What are
your mutually exclusive choices? Describe them in writing.
What actions must your group take to prepare for each choice?
Write them down.

Label and write down at least one tradeoff you soon will
be facing in your career. What are your mutually exclusive
choices? Describe them in writing. What actions must you
take to prepare for each choice? Write them down.

18

How to Refine Your Gifts

To test your *refining of your gifts,* please answer the following questions by marking the response item that most closely matches your typical behavior.

1. Do you avoid naming your *true desires* in your life, your company, your projects?
   Usually/Often _____ Sometimes/Seldom _____

2. Do you distinguish between wishes and desires?
   Usually/Often _____ Sometimes/Seldom _____

3. Do you avoid constructive drudgery in your life and work?
   Usually/Often _____ Sometimes/Seldom _____

4. Do you think of yourself as gifted?
   Usually/Often _____ Sometimes/Seldom _____

5. Do you actively cultivate your gifts?
   Usually/Often _____ Sometimes/Seldom _____

6. Do you feel sorry for yourself?
   Usually/Often _____ Sometimes/Seldom _____

7. Do you expect the world to be your cheerleader?
   Usually/Often _____ Sometimes/Seldom _____

8. Do you find failure devastating? Does failure knock you down and keep you down for too long a period?
   Usually/Often _____ Sometimes/Seldom _____

9. Do you work long hours in areas that encompass your desires?
   Usually/Often _____ Sometimes/Seldom _____

10. Do you use your gifts well to reorder your work environment—
to make an *impact* you're proud of?
Usually/Often _____ Sometimes/Seldom _____

MY REFINING YOUR GIFTS INDEX

To determine your score on the *refining your gifts* quiz, check your
answers against the correct ones listed in Appendix B.

For each correct answer, give yourself one-half point. Add
up the correct answers and mark the rating category that corresponds to your score.

My score _____   _____ Superior   4.5–5.0
(Refining Your Gifts Index) _____ Good   4.0
                             _____ Satisfactory 3.5
                             _____ Fair   3.0
                             _____ Poor   0.0–2.5

REFINING YOUR GIFTS

Desire is destiny, for good or ill. Desire's pull has an impact on our everyday lives, whether we acknowledge it or not. Elizabeth, a woman grown old in Mary Gordon's novel, *The Company of Women*, reflects on it as it pertains to the practice of her lifelong faith: "Still, I make prayers of petition because I believe one good comes of it: the expression of desire. It is important to know what one longs for, and to know it clearly; in the area of desire, one should not err." This wise woman knows that to ignore desire, or accommodate it poorly, is to invite mischief.

My friends know that I am a lover of the ocean. This prompts some to ask why I haven't taken up sailing. My reply to them is that sailing is something I wish I wanted to do. Without realizing it, when I first said this I had made the important distinction between desire and wish.

We all have wishes, but they are more a reflection of sought-after status in some circle, and the accumulation of symbolic badges of belonging and accomplishment. Should we somehow bring ourselves to act on them and make them come true, our typical experience is that they do not bring the sense of reward we're counting on.

On the other hand, identifying true desire in ourselves is the first step that leads to refining our gifts and personal fulfillment.

Responsibility and Choice

For most of us, the idea of responsibility is accompanied by a sense of obligation toward others. While there is nothing inaccurate or improper about this, such joint tenancy in our minds often obscures an important meaning of responsibility: responsibility as it applies to self. It surrounds the understanding of the *consequences* of our perceptions and choices, and how those consequences affect what we owe ourselves.

It is so very hard to be responsible to ourselves. This is

where responsibility is most painful, and we are tempted to avoid it by denying it or running from it. Being honest with ourselves about what we want and what we have to do to earn it is as difficult a responsibility as any we encounter. It requires that we lay all excuse making aside.

Facing desire squarely and truthfully is to choose personal responsibility. While doing so can set us on a course for refining our gifts, there's no escaping the demands it makes on us. We recognize that to satisfy it, we're going to have to take a run at something that is going to cost us toil and anguish. Yet accommodating desire is the only hope for bringing us more fully into harmony with ourselves.

In my comments in chapter 10 on acting on our unique strengths, I said that *caring* is the critical ingredient. In refining our gifts, the same thinking applies in that desire is necessary to refine our gifts. Possibly you think I'm splitting hairs by separating unique strengths and gifts. Though you may have your point, I choose to make this distinction: I see unique strengths as already residing in a person. They are traits, attitudes, and values that have been built up over the years, are currently present, and just need a layer or two of inhibition peeled away to be put to use. In contrast, while present in seed, gifts have to be cultivated.

When perceived accurately, desire is the fuel for fortitude. Because it is natural—not conjured up—it provides power. This is essential. Gifts are one thing. Cultivating them is quite another.

Drudgery, Drill, and Discouragement

Good ideas are not rare. How could they be? Just consider the 3,000-plus colleges and unversities in America alone, where the exploration of ideas repeatedly takes place in a myriad of settings. Then think of the large libraries on those campuses and spread throughout all our cities. Consider the laboratories and think tanks that dot the landscape and are located in our successful corporations as well. Think of all the executives and professionals whom we call on routinely for competence, imagination and innovation. Think of the centuries through which learning and thought have advanced. Good ideas—even great ones—cannot possibly be rare. But getting them to work, listened to, believed in, or acted on is rare indeed.

Gifts are not rare either. In fact, we all have them. Moreover, the world welcomes them. What the world won't be, however, is our cheerleader. It remains for us as individuals to accept the drudgery, see the purpose of drilling, and overcome our discouragement to cultivate our gifts. So while gifts themselves are not rare, people who refine them are.

An unbelabored, untormented Mozart never would have been heard of. The same could be said of countless others, including Albert Einstein, Ella Fitzgerald, Herschel Walker, and Alfred Sloan. You've probably heard the story of a man being stopped on the street in New York City by a passerby who asked him how he could get to Carnegie Hall. The man's reply was, "Practice, man, practice!"

Some people are better at overcoming discouragement than others. Whether we are better or worse at it, overcome it we must. On the way to refining our gifts, there are bound to be numerous pratfalls for us, and times when we begin to feel sorry for ourselves. Gift refinement never comes easily. What is most difficult for us, however, is when the world refuses to be our cheerleader. In fact, it is often the opposite that occurs, and those closest to us may well wonder aloud why we stick with it.

Thomas Edison is a good model for us here. Apparently he and Henry Ford—sixteen years his junior—were friends. One day Ford was visiting Edison in the laboratory where he did much of his work. Observing that Edison's drudgery had just led him to one more failure in a long series of experiments, Ford asked if Edison didn't get so discouraged that he just wanted to pack it all in. Edison's retort was an emphatic "No"; on the contrary, he had just discovered one

more way not to make his invention work, and that knowledge would be useful to him later.

Let me return to one of my personal heroes: George
Lucas, achiever *par excellence*. You will remember I referred
to him in chapter 6. This time, Lucas serves as an example
of the supreme talent who makes no mistake in understanding what is demanded of anyone who seeks to excel. He offered his views in an interview published in the May 15, 1983
Chicago Tribune. The interview, conducted by film critic Gene
Siskel, ran like this:

> *Siskel:* What do you and your friend Steven Spielberg know
> about moviemaking that the rest of Hollywood apparently
> doesn't know?
> *Lucas:* I think part of it is that we enjoy movies. We've always
> enjoyed watching movies. And we're serious about making
> them, and there's an obvious talent there. But you have to be
> dedicated and serious about it, have the talent and enjoy it.
> You have to *enjoy* making a good movie and entertaining an
> audience. And both Steven and I are like that. We like ex-
> pressing things filmically. But a lot of people are in the film
> business for the status and for the money, but when it comes
> down to actually making the movie, they don't really care
> that much.
>
> But Steven and I have that commitment. As you can see
> I can't sort of halfway make a movie. That's why I'm stopping
> for a while. I can't do it halfway and work nine to five and
> come home and party. I have to work on the movie on Sunday
> and I know Steve is the same way. Steve can deal with it
> because he doesn't have a family.
> *Siskel:* Do you have any advice to kids in college who want to
> be like you and Spielberg?
> *Lucas:* Well, everyone to his own self has to be true. You either
> have the talent or you don't. And you shouldn't worry about
> that part. But most important, they shouldn't be afraid to
> work long hours because that's what it takes. You're going
> to have to commit your life to it. You can't expect somebody
> to hand you a finished film on a platter. It's going to take a
> lot of hard, hard work and dedication. A lot of people don't
> understand that. They think it just sort of happens. And they're

always amazed at how much work is involved and what the real standards are.
Siskel: Did you have a teacher who taught you that?
Lucas: No, I just sort of came to it naturally. In film school I just loved it so much that it became a 24-hour-a-day thing with me. And only after I was finally able to get a film off the ground did I realize just how much hard work was a key ingredient. You just have to put in the time and energy.

The late Dorothy Parker, one of our first-rate writers, said, "I hate writing, but I love having written." She opens the way to an important realization. Drudgery and drill expose us to the opportunity of inspiration that is fueled by our desire and provided by our gifts.

Reordering the Workplace

"Genius, in truth, means little more than the faculty of perceiving in an unhabitual way." With these words, William James underscored the notion that it is how resourceful we are with our gifts, rather than the gifts themselves, that is of greatest substance.

Many executives, including chief executives, are inclined not to think of themselves as having gifts, but of being "merely managers." That is, they rightly pride themselves on knowing how to get things done through other people. However, while managing people *superbly* is a display of gifts on the job, these executives err first of all, by not thinking of themselves as gifted, and second, by not developing those gifts enough to make the most out of their work environment.

To repeat, it is in *acknowledging* desire that an executive sets the direction in refining his gifts. And it is in setting a direction that an executive begins to reorder his environment in such a way that it not only accommodates, but enhances his movement toward his sought-after destination. As simplistic, naive, and self-centered as acknowledging desire may appear, it produces new energy and renders the executive fresh in spirit, noticeably more resourceful to peers and superiors, and more self-assured to subordinates.

The refining of one's gifts leads to the reduction of routine, ordinariness, and mediocrity. It leads to an executive's upside-down look at everything and everybody in his surroundings. Examples of gifts executives have that need refinement are conceiving, interpreting, building, rallying, steadying, inspiring, designing, deciding, persuading, writing, speaking, planning, predicting, perceiving, organizing, trusting, simplifying, committing, and adventuring.

No executive possesses all of these gifts, but he or she will be the owner of some of them plus others not mentioned. Within them lie the means to mastery in some way. Therein also lies the opportunity to utilize the work environment, to see *for the first time* (remember William James) elements in it that can be used in a startling way to serve the executive's initiatives and bring about creative solutions.

Just as a young person with the gift of perception and a bent toward healing must undergo the rigors of medical training and residency before he becomes a psychiatrist, so must a young trainee with the gift of persuasion undergo the disciplines of training and lengthy experience before he becomes a foremost sales executive. The ahead-of-the-pack executive with a natural adventuresomeness must blend countless knocks, disappointments, and successes over many years into a broad, deepening experience before he is prepared to lead some company on a consistent course for growth. The executive with a natural trust must learn to temper it so that he prudently delegates only to those who truly thrive on it.

If such examples seem mundane, simply think for a moment of how many failed executives you know who would have succeeded if they were "just a little bit better" at this or that. Then think of how the "this and that" are most often intangible, personal qualities. Then remember, as a further example, that in a four-round championship golf tournament, only one stroke usually separates the winner from the rest of the contenders. Finally, imagine all that went into the development of that victor's poise.

What needs to be kept in mind is that desire, which resides in whatever gifts we are fortunate to possess, is only fuel. It is evidence that the gift is natural. However, it is patiently and minutely refining gifts over an entire life and career that sets the achiever apart from the wishful thinker. This is the mark of the truly matured executive.

The type of executive associates shake their heads at in positive wonderment is the one who does distinctive things in captivating ways. Such is the executive who has refined (and continues to refine) his gifts. Refined gifts are deceptive. They make their expression look easy. It has been said that the reason Bing Crosby was so successful was because he made his listeners think *they* could sing. In other words, he made it look effortless.

We don't dare believe it! Crosby's achievement in entertainment—as is true with all accomplished persons—was bought at the high price of lifelong total commitment to refine his gifts.

If we are to live up to our potential by any measure, the same is required of us.

WRITTEN ACTION PLAN

Suggestions for changing your thought and behavior patterns to raise your *refining your gifts* index.

1. Sit back in your chair, relax, and for a few minutes let your mind do some scanning. Without placing any judgment ("good" or "bad") on what you generate, jot down what you believe to be your true desires. Do not limit yourself only to desires concerning work, but include those for any and all spheres of your life. Write down all that float across your mind.

Now go back over your list, and very, very carefully examine each item to conclude whether it is a true desire or merely a wish. If an item is a wish, draw a line through it.

To ignore these desires, or accommodate them poorly, is to invite mischief into your life. They are the fuel for refining your gifts. In turn, a gift is a tool for experiencing the fruits of desire.

2. Repeat the process above, except this time list what you believe to be your gifts: abilities-in-seed that come to you naturally; abilities that if cultivated would set you apart from others in achievement.

Now count up the number of desires you have and draw that many columns on a sheet of paper. At the top of each column, write down one of those desires. Beneath each desire list your gifts, which if cultivated would help satisfy that desire.

3. Do you fool yourself into thinking that the really good and lasting things in life "just sort of happen"? "Breaks" happen. "Chance" happens. But the generating of life-themes and their climaxes don't. They are arrived at after long journeys. And even then, the "climax" turns out to be a plateau on a journey to a greater consciousness.

Choose one desire you mustn't deny any longer. Write it down. Notice the gifts you must cultivate to experience the fruits of that desire. Get on with the drill and the drudgery. Stick with it and learn the meaning of inspiration.

Review your written action plan for chapter 12, "Setting Priorities: Finding Holes, Setting Goals, and Creating Roles," to see if you need to revise any goals set there.

19

Today's Management Model: The Facilitator

BEING A FACILITATOR QUIZ

To test your *being a facilitator,* please answer the following questions by marking the response item that most closely matches your typical behavior.

1. Do you see yourself as a willing participant in a collaborative management process?
   Usually/Often _____ Sometimes/Seldom _____

2. Do you resent the increasing predominance of the collaborative management process prior to decision making?
   Usually/Often _____ Sometimes/Seldom _____

3. Do you think your job does not provide you with enough to do?
   Usually/Often _____ Sometimes/Seldom _____

4. Do you observe the abilities and interests of a wide range of people in your entire company with an eye to how they might join with you on some project?
   Usually/Often _____ Sometimes/Seldom _____

5. Do you believe you make clear to others in the company that you would be available to help them in projects they might undertake?
   Usually/Often _____ Sometimes/Seldom _____

6. Do you believe your associates think of you as a team player?
   Usually/Often _____ Sometimes/Seldom _____

7. Do you suffer from the "not invented here" syndrome?
Usually/Often _____ Sometimes/Seldom _____

8. Do you hog credit that should go to subordinates and peers?
Usually/Often _____ Sometimes/Seldom _____

9. Are you committed to encouraging your associates to act on their unique strengths?
Usually/Often _____ Sometimes/Seldom _____

10. Are you good at distinguishing when you should lead, follow, or get out of the way?
Usually/Often _____ Sometimes/Seldom _____

MY BEING A FACILITATOR INDEX

To determine your score on the *being a facilitator* quiz, check your answers against the correct ones listed in Appendix B.

For each correct answer, give yourself one-half point. Add up the correct answers and mark the rating category that corresponds to your score.

My score _____   _____ Superior   4.5–5.0
(Being a Facilitator Index)   _____ Good   4.0
                                   _____ Satisfactory   3.5
                                   _____ Fair   3.0
                                   _____ Poor   0.0–2.5

BEING A FACILITATOR

In the Introduction, I said that the achiever is someone who
gets the right things done. Most important is the fact that
he or she gets them done through others. In short, the modern
achiever is a facilitator.

Facilitator is a word that has gained most use in the
behavioral sciences, and more specifically, in the group encounter movement. Its use in business has sprung mainly
from early experiments with the so-called "sensitivity training" methods of the late fifties and sixties that were conducted by the National Training Laboratories. NTL, an agency
of the National Education Association, held these training
sessions at its campground in Bethel, Maine. Many of our
most successful corporations supported and participated in
their programs.

These sensitivity-training experiments were carried out
among small groups of executives who were in attendance
to learn how to become more sensitive to the meaning of the
behavior of those who surround them, and in general, to
develop their skills for fostering and excelling in a more par-
ticipative management climate.

What was most distinctive about these experimental
groups was that they were "leaderless." That is, they were
not dominated by an authority figure who took upon him or
herself the responsibility for the direction of the group. Present in each group, however, was a trained behavioral scientist who served as a coordinator or consultant to the group.
His purpose was to help the group question and understand
its processes, but not tell it what to do. Over the years, these
and other such persons who were similarly involved in the
fast-growing group-learning field throughout all professions,
most often came to be called facilitators.

Business became disenchanted with sensitivity training,
as well it might, because its efforts took place in a somewhat
clinical atmosphere, while the atmosphere of business most

decidedly is not. In other words, the training experience didn't travel well. Nonetheless, business owes a debt to sensitivity training because it called attention to the need for new skills among executives at a time when it became clear to all but the most bullying types that collaboration was fast becoming the predominant means of generating initiatives and developing decision alternatives.

The job facing achievers today is not to debate the merits or demerits of group action versus individual action. That issue is settled. Collaborative management is here—to stay. The task at hand is to make it work well.

Astute Selector of Associates
The fact that collaborative management is here to stay is a good reason to return to the notion that the achiever approaches his work and career with a task-force mentality. The task force is tailor-made for today's collaborative climate (I have more to say about that in Appendix A IV), but what I want to point out here is that the attitudes and disciplines required to make a task force work can be applied on the job every day.

One of the most important disciplines employed to make a task force work is to ensure that the right people are selected and recruited to serve on it. Although an executive occupies a "box" on the company's organization chart, and that box "reports" to another box or boxes that likewise have occupants obligated to conform to detailed job descriptions, an executive has a great deal of leeway in taking initiative on what she or he will tackle and *with whom.*

There isn't an achiever alive who doesn't realize that his job—if he approaches it with a positive attitude—is bigger than he can handle. That is, if he were to try to carry out all the elements of his job description in the manner prescribed therein, he would have to put in a 24-hour day, seven days a week, and he would still not get it done. The key, then, is for him to select for his effort those areas that are most important to the company and where superior performance by him will have the most impact. Then he looks around the organization (anywhere and everywhere) to find those people—if he can attract them to his project—whose contributions will help assure him of turning in a superior performance.

Astute spotting of people whose abilities and interests applied to a job can spell the difference between mediocrity and excellence takes hard thought and imagination. Then it has to be followed up with persuasion; selling another on the worth of the undertaking and emphasizing that that person's "full-throttle" contribution will be highly valued. In return, the recruiting achiever offers his talents in kind. He assures each of the collaborators whose services he seeks that he stands ready to offer his own services to them on projects where they can be put to singular advantage.

The executive who expresses his desire to initiate and join such collaborations makes it clear throughout the organization that he is an imaginative and resourceful team player.

The Invisible Initiator
Whether those who have been recruited to collaborate with the achiever on a project are from outside his department, or work with him every day, he needs to remember this is just the critical first step in getting distinctive things done. While assembling a first-rate team—no matter how loosely or informally linked—is no mean feat, what is required of the assembler is that he now take on a more low-key approach toward initiative. Adroitness in this endeavor is what makes him a true facilitator.

The achiever-facilitator knows full well that the "not invented here" syndrome is a killer for future initiatives. Moreover, he also realizes that another sin he absolutely must not commit is that of taking credit for the ideas and accomplishments that grow out of the joint efforts of the work group he has assembled. So not only does he refuse to be jealous of good ideas and performance of others, he also insists that credit for accomplishment go to his group even if it is generally thought those accomplishments stemmed from his urging and brain.

The facilitator well may take firm stands or strongly espouse a cause that provokes quick and equally vehement counterreactions from his associates. Sometimes his stands are ones he believes in deeply. Other times, he may be voicing them primarily to elicit thoughts and actions from a group that is languishing at dead center. Sometimes he scolds. Mostly he praises. Always he encourages. And those encouragements are for initiatives currently being taken and *yet* to be taken by *others*. The presence of the facilitating achiever is seen and felt by the questions he asks and the encouragement he offers. But the purpose of those questions and encouragements is to get the members of the work group he has assembled to act on their unique strengths. It is to question ideas *they* have generated, to gain clarification within the group, and to encourage action on initiatives *they* have conceived. The time may come when he will be called upon to make a decision, and it will be his job to choose from alternatives, all of which were generated by *them*. In this sense, the facilitator is invisible.

Leader and Follower

The large accounting firm of Deloitte Haskins & Sells sends out a weekly newsletter to its clients titled, appropriately enough, *The Week In Review*. It is a compendium of tax, accounting, and various financial matters that are pertinent to the concerns of executives responsible for managing the assets of their corporations. One of the features that appears without fail at the tail end of each newsletter is "Thought for the Week." This is the part of *The Week In Review* I enjoy most. One of these that appeared a couple of years ago tickled me and bears special relevance to the topic of this chapter. It read: "Lead, follow or get out of the way!"

As I mentioned, the facilitator asks the right questions, takes positions, and elicits the best, unfiltered thoughts from the group he has assembled. These actions are based on his judgments, convictions, and exercise of vision. In these areas, he serves as a leader. However, if he has done his job right as a selector and assembler of talented and committed associates, he is bound to be a follower. His role in this case is as a supporter and willing hand who pitches in with the work that emerges.

John Naisbitt, author of *Megatrends*, has his tongue only slightly in cheek when he says that a leader is someone who finds a parade and jumps in front of it. More seriously, he says that the true leader today is a facilitator; someone who serves as catalyst in getting people to work together to achieve some goal of worth. Obviously, I couldn't agree more. The facilitator is a leader first and foremost in *communication*, but when it comes to execution, he is a follower, and he should be the best follower he can possibly be.

WRITTEN ACTION PLAN

Suggestions for changing your thought and action to raise your *being a facilitator* index.

1. Think of fifteen talented peers and subordinates throughout your company with whom you have had some contact. In making your selections, pay no attention to what department or group they are a part of, and, likewise disregard their functional specialty. For example, if you are a marketing executive, feel free to include manufacturing, accounting, or any other types in your thinking. However, if people from your department or specialty come to mind, do not exclude them. List all fifteen names.

Consider a project you have just agreed to take on, or plan to take on, where superior performance by you will have an impact on the company. Review your list to see which people on it might be willing to join your temporary, collaborative, interdisciplinary effort. Place a check mark beside their names.

- ○ Note what specific strengths or gifts of each make her or him fitting for the project.
- ○ Write out what you must do to make your project attractive to each.
- ○ Write out what you will have to offer in return (now or later) for her or his contribution.
- ○ Make good on what you offer.

Note: If your project is one to be attended to strictly within your department, this process is equally applicable, and you only need direct your recruitment considerations to strengths and gifts of those within your discipline.

2. List three occasions in the past year when you have rejected worthwhile ideas or initiatives from others for seemingly plausible reasons, but when your rejection could be described more accurately as a cropping up of the "not invented here" syndrome.

If in fact you have made this error, resolve not to repeat it.

3. List three occasions in the past year when you have hogged credit that rightfully should have gone to others.

If in fact you have made this error, resolve not to repeat it.

Read Appendix A IV.

20

Exercising Vision:
What It Is, What It Isn't

EXERCISING VISION QUIZ

To test your *exercising of vision*, please answer the following questions by marking the response item that most closely matches your typical behavior.

1. Do you believe you are thought of by your associates as a person characterized by a "special seeing"?
Usually/Often _____ Sometimes/Seldom _____

2. Do you look for "signs and symbols" (in addition to rhetoric and stated objectives) in your corporation that indicate what form and direction it will take in the future?
Usually/Often _____ Sometimes/Seldom _____

3. Do you *study* the "rewards and punishments" distributed in your company to determine where it is headed, what type of "personality" it has, what are the characteristics of its "culture"?
Usually/Often _____ Sometimes/Seldom _____

4. Do you feel harried in carrying out your job responsibilities?
Usually/Often _____ Sometimes/Seldom _____

5. Whether or not "long-range" or "strategic" planning is taken seriously in your company, do *you* give thought to what it will be doing twenty-five years from now?
Usually/Often _____ Sometimes/Seldom _____

6. Do you believe lengthy, repeated discussions with your associates prior to reaching important decisions is inefficient?
Usually/Often _____ Sometimes/Seldom _____

7. Do you associate vision with charismatic people?
   Usually/Often _____   Sometimes/Seldom _____

8. Do you make a distinction between mass charisma and face-to-face charisma?
   Usually/Often _____   Sometimes/Seldom _____

9. Do you assume dramatic change follows the exercise of vision?
   Usually/Often _____   Sometimes/Seldom _____

10. Do you believe vision is a rare "gift" that stands all by itself; that one either "has it" or doesn't?
    Usually/Often _____   Sometimes/Seldom _____

MY EXERCISING VISION INDEX

To determine your score on the *exercising vision* quiz, check your answers against the correct ones listed in Appendix B.

For each correct answer, give yourself one-half point. Add up the correct answers and mark the rating category that corresponds to your score.

My score _____   _____ Superior   4.5–5.0
(Exercising Vision Index)   _____ Good   4.0
                               _____ Satisfactory   3.5
                               _____ Fair   3.0
                               _____ Poor   0.0–2.5

EXERCISING VISION

When critics of the American corporation set about their task in earnest, one of the first indictments they level at the corporation's performance is that it displays a lack of vision. They have their point, to be sure. The ramifications of such a shortcoming are underscored matter-of-factly in a memorable Old Testament passage that says, "Where there is no vision, the people perish."

Yet the call for "vision," as with the call for "leadership," is largely a shibboleth; a drummer-up of emotion and "principle," but virtually meaningless. Lack of corporate vision usually is linked in criticism with the corporation's neglect of taking a long-range view. But that is about as far as most critics go in articulating what vision means, and what actually is demanded of corporations and their executives who seek to exercise vision.

Certainly the exercise of vision has its ultimate payoff in the future. However, plans for the future cannot be enacted without taking steps in the present, and realizing in what ways the decisions and actions of today have an impact on a corporation's faraway tomorrow. Keeping in mind my comments in chapter 17 about how the "parts emerge in anticipation of the whole," vision is perceiving how the events, actions, and thoughts of the present are omens—good and bad—of what lies ahead. Vision is a *special seeing* that comprehends the order of things that do not meet the ordinary eye. It is a special seeing by some that makes connections others miss. It is a special seeing that allows those who exercise it to call attention to *what-we-are-now* as a sign of *what-we-are-going-to-be*. Then we can do whatever we choose to enhance that movement if we want it, or redirect it if we do not. Such special seeing is a mark of the achiever.

Breadth and Depth
Exercising vision is exercising vigilance in the here and now. Abundant time and energy invested in discerning the *purpose*

of such matters as rhetoric, thought, plans, decisions, methods, emphases, promotions, firings, workstyle—in short, the sum of values and behavior in one's own executive suite and business life in general—is required if one is to sense where a corporation is headed. Such a sense grows out of an *appetite for exploring events and actions* in and around a corporation in their breadth and depth.

Most executives will snort at the notion that they must be vigilant about the here and now. "What else is there?" they ask. Indeed, many feel so harried about what they are expected to do in the present that they find the idea of long-range planning a startlingly romantic notion. However, the problem with our absorption with getting things done in the present is that it often is narrow and shallow. This absorption often translates to Band-Aid performance—postponing problems in the service of today's opportunism—and adopting a perspective that is, to use a term of Marshall McLuhan, "rear-view-mirror."

I am not one to glamorize the management practices of the Japanese. I believe that has been overdone, and that before long the Japanese will again have much to learn from us. However, there is one area of their business practice that I find admirable. Predictably enough, it is one we Americans chide them for. That practice is for the upper echelons of their corporate management seemingly to talk a subject to death before reaching a decision on it. This phenomenon led one of my friends to quip, "Japanese management has a long digestive tract."

Beautiful metaphor. What we American executives often do *not* do is digest. We handle. Quickly. We worship at the altar of fast decision making. But issues and actions with significant ramifications do not *pass through us*. We don't *think*. We don't ask apparently absurd questions to see if we can discover profound connections and relationships in the order of things. We don't think because we don't have the time. We're too busy *doing*.

What the Japanese method (that we find so inefficient) produces is quality *communication*. It generates an inquiring disposition and fertile, inclusive thought. And what it eliminates are inappropriate goals and false starts. We Americans are known by our false starts and changed courses. While the Japanese are slow to reach decisions, their decisions tend to be more "true" than ours with the result that their *execution* is more efficient than ours.

Vision and Charisma

Charisma is a funny thing, wouldn't you say? And elusive, too. We revere it as a concept. Franklin Roosevelt, John Kennedy, Martin Luther King, Jr., and Ronald Reagan. Definitely good. But what about Jim Jones and Adolf Hitler? They were charismatic too. Definitely bad.

The concept of charisma as we know it came from the German scholar, Max Weber. What we call charisma came out of his theoretical discussion of what he termed "charismatic authority." He distinguished charismatic authority from rational or traditional authority. He clearly believed— and I assume most of us agree with him—that charisma is a necessity in a leader when we face legitimate rapid change (not novelty). However, he laboriously pointed out that charisma can be downright dangerous to *order*, or to consistency and routine when they are the requirements of the day. The way he put it was: "Both rational and traditional authority are specifically forms of everyday routine control of action; while the charismatic type is the direct antithesis of this."

Vision and charisma often are linked in the popular mentality much as vision and taking the long-range view. This misconception can lead us astray with disastrous results. Many charismatic people have virtually no vision. Some do. Many noncharismatic people have virtually no vision. Some do. In short, vision and charisma are not automatically a hand-and-glove operation.

Then there is a mass kind of charisma to be contrasted

with face-to-face or small-group charisma. Some people are charismatic in all settings. Some are charismatic in one or another. Some are charismatic in neither. But again, the main issue to address is which of these people have vision and are willing to exercise it. And what is more important to grasp is that vision is the far more essential quality, because whether change or routine is the order of the day, *the exercise of vision is what determines the thought and action appropriate to the current state of affairs.* Contrary to popular thought, vision is not the automatic adversary of routine and tradition. They undeniably have their place. The person of vision knows this.

Vision and Commitment
In chapter 13, I stated my view that tenacity is a critical element of an executive's showing good judgment. That indicates, to my mind at least, that since exercising vision contributes to the rendering of good judgment, tenacity and vision are bedfellows. To be sure, the executive with vision hangs in there, and it is important to remember that he or she hangs in *now*, because hanging in now is what the future is all about! (With no good today, there's no right tomorrow.) On the other hand, being committed today carries the responsibility of *staying* committed tomorrow. This responsibility is an arduous, taxing one. But it also is exhilarating and one borne eagerly by the true achiever.

Whether you like him or not, or agree with him or not, Ronald Reagan strikes me as a person of vision. He also happens to be charismatic, which helped get him elected. But he's nothing if not committed. You may not like his ideas, but he has been committed to them for a long time. And rather than finding a parade and jumping in front of it, as John Naisbitt says leaders do, Mr. Reagan seems to have hung in place until the parade caught up with him. Moreover, his commitment has been tested repeatedly in that he has been called the equivalent of a philosophical, social, and political dinosaur in some of our most respectable circles. Nonetheless, when the invective and adversarial political rhetoric has evaporated, I think it will be clear that he was a president who got a lot done. Only time will tell if what he got done is good for the country.

It is fitting to conclude this book with the consideration of vision. This is so because the exercise of vision entails the combination of many traits that I have written about in some of the preceding chapters. For example, exercising vision requires not only tenacity, but, among other traits, the willingness to be vulnerable, the practice of thinking positively, and the wisdom to make bold and judicious decisions. Most important, however, is realizing that exercising vision is the expression of honesty and courage far more than it is a rare "gift" that stands all by itself.

In the last analysis, *exercising vision is the practice of resourcefulness*. Wise perception—a special seeing—has a way of inspiring one's associates to act on their unique strengths. It serves as a catalyst and integrator—a unifier. It reduces wasted motion. Exercising vision gets the right things done. And in keeping with the makeup of the modern achiever, it gets them done through others.

WRITTEN ACTION PLAN

Suggestions for changing your thought and action to raise your *exercising vision* index.

1. Think back over your work experiences the past five years. Think of three major projects that had company-wide attention and support from top management, yet flopped.

Employing hindsight, write down what goals of each project may have been inappropriate for your company to adopt. Also write down what false starts, if any, were made on each project.

Now consider one major project in which you are currently engaged. Review its goals. Have you and your associates been too busy *doing* to exercise vision? Have you looked at yourselves as to how "what-we-are-now" is a sign of "what-we-are-going-to-be" and determined if this "fits" your corporate culture? Is "what-we-are-going-to-be" good?

In your view have you defined your *problem* accurately? Have you dug deep to explore all the alternatives? Have you weighed all their consequences? Have you made a "true" decision? Are you ready for efficient execution?

Read *The Mind of the Organization* by Ben Heirs and Gordon Pehrson (Harper & Row, 1982). This excellent small book deals with these latter topics clearly and simply. It will be helpful to you.

2. Learn to spot the pretenders from the people of vision, and learn how to exercise vision by associating with and emulating the latter.

- ○ Write down the names of five charismatic executives who impressed you as people of vision when you first met them, but later disappointed you.

- ○ What actions of each wore thin?

- ○ Write down the names of five executives who were not impressive to you at first, but later turned out to be people of vision.

- ○ What actions of each impressed you?

3. What "parades" do you believe are coming that perhaps you should "hang in there" for?

Name two and write out what you must do to prepare for their arrival.

MY RESOURCEFULNESS INDEX

To determine your *resourcefulness index,* add up your scores from the quizzes listed below. Then mark the rating category that corresponds to your score.

Delivering the Goods   _____

Thinking Beyond the   _____
Obvious

Refining Your Gifts   _____

Being a Facilitator   _____

Exercising Vision   _____

My Resourcefulness Index   _____

_____ Superior   22.5–25.0

_____ Good   20.0–22.0

_____ Satisfactory   17.5–19.5

_____ Fair   15.0–17.0

_____ Poor   0.0–14.5

MY ACHIEVER INDEX

To determine your complete *achiever index,* add up your scores
for each of the four qualities listed below. Then mark the rating
category that corresponds to your score.

Other-Centered   _____

Courageous   _____

Judicious   _____

Resourceful   _____

My Achiever Index   _____

_____ Superior   90–100

_____ Good   80–89

_____ Satisfactory   70–79

_____ Fair   60–69

_____ Poor   0.0–59

THE PLEDGE: COMMITMENT NOW!

YOU HAVE JUST completed a thorough achiever-development program and computed your ACHIEVER INDEX. If your ACHIEVER INDEX is high and you have been candid with yourself in answering the quizzes, you have reason to be proud of your performance. Whatever you're doing, keep doing it!

If your ACHIEVER INDEX is not as high as you would like it to be, make a commitment to complete the exercises at the end of each chapter where your scores are the lowest. Putting those *Written Action Plans* into practice is sure to improve your executive performance, raise your scores on retaking the quizzes, and make you more the achiever you seek to be.

Such commitment made *now* is what this book has been about. And whether you're well on your way as a true achiever, or just starting this "journey of a thousand miles that begins with one step," unqualified commitment is what you must produce.

If you're willing to make this commitment now, you're ready for THE 10-POINT PLEDGE OF THE ACHIEVER . . .

THE 10-POINT PLEDGE OF THE ACHIEVER

1. Today I will greet at least three people warmly and geniunely.

2. Today I will perform a task of which I am proud.

3. This week I will encourage someone to stretch him or herself and offer my assistance to that process wherever appropriate.

4. This week, if called for, I will make a bold, judicious decision.

5. This week I will start or complete reading a book or article that is not directly related to my career.

6. This month I will win approval from my boss to fill a hole in our organization's efforts where I can call upon my unique strengths.

7. This month, and at least once each year, I will take action in some area that I care about where I have yet to succeed.

8. This month, and twelve months from now, I will set two strenuous *one-year* goals for myself. One will require primarily my individual effort; the other primarily a group effort.

9. This month, and thirty-six months from now, I will set a strenuous *three-year* goal for myself.

10. I will set no goal that I cannot achieve, nor will I serve systems. I will see to it that the systems of which I am a part serve *people*.

The three by-words of the achiever are:

HOLES

GOALS

ROLES

The achiever:

> FINDS THE FIRST
>
>> SETS THE SECOND
>>
>>> CREATES THE THIRD

In the last analysis the achiever is a *giver*.

He gives to his work what he does to his *whole life;* namely, some of what he owes, much of what he fears, and all of what he cares about most deeply.

BUREAUCRACY AND THE ACHIEVER

It is remarkable that knowledge of the essentials of human behavior is so poorly disseminated and translated into action. . . . In the most rigorous and technically elegant structures, the weakest bit is still the softest and most familiar—people.

LIONEL TIGER

IN CHAPTER 10, I stated that it is well known we do not give expression to our unique strengths in a vacuum. I further stated that for us as executives, that translates to the corporate organization and its particular environment. Whereas the body of this book deals with the making of the achiever, this appendix deals with the relationship between the achiever and the organization. In particular, I call attention to that aspect of corporate organization we call bureaucracy, and describe some elements of the impact it and the achiever have on each other. Finally, I offer some observations on how corporations may reduce the more dehumanizing and frustrating effects of bureaucracy, not on just their existing achievers, but on their entire work force—many of whom would be achievers.

I

Bureaucracy: Another Look at an Old Nemesis

My favorite college professor had a way with words. He taught sociology and was aware that many concepts in his field defied easy understanding. When we students addressed such a concept in class one day, he summed up our frustration at "getting it" by saying, "This is a little like trying to pin custard pie to the wall."

That's what most would-be achievers think when they view corporate bureaucracy with an eye to how it can serve them better. To be sure, bureaucracy can be defined easily enough: a large-scale division of labor to perform defined tasks. But understanding the way it actually works and doesn't work is another matter.

Such understanding is difficult because one often forgets he or she is marshal as well as minion within bureaucracy. Yet assessment is what is required to discern the essential aspects of bureaucracy from those that merely seem so and are dehumanizing. There is a need for us all to help rally those top managements who believe that unless they reduce the dehumanizing elements of bureaucracy, their companies—no matter what their growth in size—eventually will lose the ability to serve their markets and court death.

The May 5, 1980 issue of *Fortune* was a significant one. It was the silver anniversary of the first publication of the five hundred largest industrial corporations. It compared the original 1955 ranking of the Fortune 500 largest industrial corporations with that of 1980. In an article entitled "Twenty-Five Years of Change in the Fortune 500," the editors noted that 238 companies appearing on that 1955 list did not make the 1980 lineup. Two hundred and sixty-two companies still remain on the list. One hundred and eighty-five have been absorbed by merger. Twenty-nine are now too small to be included. Fourteen are not considered "industrial." Six are privately held. Four are out of business entirely. Taken together, these numbers are a dramatic statement of corporate obsolescence and demise.

Fallen Giants

We need to remember that scores of once-mighty corporations are no longer with us. When we realize that business history has a littered landscape of companies that adhered to yesterday's strategies instead of adapting to change, not far behind is another, more puzzling realization. It is the one I commented on in my opening remarks in Section I. That is, while change is unarguably occurring at faster rates than in the past, it still is not at a rate beyond our *ability* to handle. As I said, the change we face is evolutionary. Nonetheless, failure to deal with it is commonplace, with predictable results.

Corporations die when they don't make enough profit to justify continued investment. Ordinarily, this occurs when their products or services are on the way out, and their leaders lack either the insight or willingness to adapt to changing circumstances. We all know instances of this kind of business mortality. The details of such pathology have been rehearsed in conversations with bereaved former employees, corporate victims themselves, or with competitors, who first looked on with relish, then fear that they might suffer the same fate.

While for most of us the spectacle of corporate death is sad, there are others who rightly will say that in a way it's also invigorating, because it reaffirms one of our notions of capitalism. That is, the corporation unable to adapt to change deserves its fate—the quicker the better—and makes way for corporations better suited for survival. Moreover, even though a corporation in its final death throes may concern us, it is not the kind of dying that should capture the bulk of our attention. Rather, we need to be vigilant about detecting disease among the living today instead of confirming it among the dead tomorrow.

It is the dread of such failure that prods us to give our best efforts to the day-to-day vitality of our own corporations. As a result of busying ourselves so sincerely, we usually come to think that failure is deserved among the incompetent and slothful. In any event, it is most certainly something we dare not anticipate happening to us! We want to believe that hard, intelligent work is all that is necessary to sustain the life of our enterprises.

Just as in our own lives, then, corporate death is something we know about, but only at the edge of awareness. We well-adjusted, unmorbid folks devote ourselves to the task of living, and our corporations to the task of thriving—and of facing new problems with new solutions.

The Zombie Corporation

That a mismanaged, outmoded, underfinanced company gets sick and dies is not surprising. But that a *seemingly healthy* corporation, with expanding markets, profits, and cash should be called sick somehow escapes our comprehension. Do you recall the popularity of those countless Boris Karloff zombie movies of the thirties? Do you remember what they were about? It wasn't the dead lying in their graves (bless their souls) who were the reason for our concern; rather, it was those stubborn, diabolical creatures who befuddled our expectations of what appropriate corpselike behavior was— and persisted in walking about terrorizing the neighborhood, thwarting most attempts to get them to lie still in a manner befitting the dead. And here's what's important: while the zombie in natural life may have been a sweet, vulnerable, unphysical type; in unnatural, zombie life he becomes invulnerable, superpowerful, and ruthless.

It seemed that in the energy flow chart that described the passage from human being to zombie, the departure of the human spirit converted to a buttressing of the flesh. What meek, compassionate, frustrated humanity could not and would not do, mindless, cold, invulnerable sinew and muscle could and would. The parallel I'm drawing points to this: it is the disparity between the *apparent* metabolic success of the corporate organism and its more debilitating dysfunctions that we should address. This can be done only by dredging up familiar issues relating to that old custard-pie-nemesis of bureaucracy. Moreover, we cannot attempt to resolve these issues unless we realize how and why bureaucracy functions the way it does.

A Valid Criticism
The critics of American corporate life who have never worked in it, or those who are so closed-minded about its value that they heap all of humanity's ills on it, are just flat out tiresome. However, there is a criticism thrust at the corporation today that I consider worthy of our utmost attention. It gives insight into the ways that living corporations die, or what's even less attractive—like the zombies—join the ranks of the walking dead.

The criticism I'm referring to deals with bureaucracy, and goes like this: *Bureaucracy so compartmentalizes enterprise that even the most intelligent and dedicated managers are prevented from understanding the final purposes of their tasks. Accordingly, such managers lose a sense of coherence and their duties become mechanical and boring. In such an environment, what else could possibly happen but that motivation withers, talent is smothered, and new blood is lost either by attrition or firing?*

This criticism concerns me for two reasons: First, because in many ways it isn't justified. Second, because in other ways, it is. So I would like to debunk parts of this criticism that often serve as an evasion of personal responsibility, and then show how such criticism *is* justified, and what might be done about it.

Rose-Colored Glasses

No reflective person would deny the need for bureaucratic structures in all large corporations. Nor could he deny the resentment they invariably prompt. However, their practical necessity supersedes the resentment to be borne. Such ill will finds its most common expression in the griping of bureaucrats, many of whom, frankly, are well fitted for what they're doing. They are not achievers.

One of the most astute thinkers about the corporate way of doing things is Wilbert Moore. In his book, *The Conduct of the Corporation,* he says, "An administrative organization is not established or continued for vague purposes of friendly interaction, but rather for objectives which can be clearly stipulated and the degree of achievement constantly or periodically appraised. Such organizations are generally badly equipped to fulfill all of life's functions or their members' interests. But they are equipped to accomplish limited functions that require complex cooperation. If more than one objective is part of the mission, it is unlikely that all can simultaneously be 'maximized' in all situations so that a priority ordering is needed as the basis for choice in cramped quarters."

In short, what Moore is saying is that bureaucratic structure may fulfill the business objectives of a corporation without fulfilling the life plan of its individual members. This is an unchangeable fact of corporate life. Critics who claim that this alone contains the seeds of corporate death have a rose-colored notion of human nature and an impractical notion of the limits of what corporations can and should do.

It is always tempting to try to harmonize individual freedom and corporate discipline, and to do the same with individual fulfillment and economic necessity. There's nothing wrong with that. In fact, we should urge the adoption of such lofty ambitions among ourselves whenever and wherever we can. However, we always need to keep in mind that the very bureaucrats whose complaints have sparked such ambitions will think us hopelessly naive, irrelevant, and self-indulgent to harbor these sentiments.

We take delight in those unusual, courageous, imaginative achievers who refuse to accept a dull corporate existence. The twenty chapters of this book, as you well know, are a "celebration" of what makes them tick. They are bent on self-development and know that to be happy they must be effective. (As Peter Drucker says, the essence of being an effective executive is to make one's strengths productive.) But while we applaud such achievers who take responsibility for their own lives and accomplishments, there seems little question that routine, protection from final responsibility, unearned luxury, ritual griping among like-minded pals, a narrowing of vision and foreshortening of horizons are just what a majority of corporate complainers at the executive level are most content to live with. That they complain in comfort is one benefit; that they avoid facing their own lack of resourcefulness and inertia is another.

The Patterns of Bureaucracy

A complex organization's need for efficiency, uniformity, and the prevention of corruption generates the characteristic mode of bureaucracy: formality which tends to be impersonal, an inflexible chain of command, promotion and influence by tenure, and special pleading by department. And it is out of these bureaucratic patterns that the most common criticisms of the system stem: rigidity, pigeonholing of responsibility, and splitting of allegiance where the bureaucrat cherishes his own role over the corporation's purpose in assigning it to him.

Despite these flaws, many bureaucrats are suited to their jobs. It seems "elitist" and a disparagement of their characters to say so, but if it is, it's not all that serious. The majority of mankind show that they are not eager for risky tasks and decisions. However—and here's the rub—they usually recognize that within their organizations there are top-level people who do assume such tasks and make such decisions. It is human to complain about their observed inequality, and just as human to blame "the system" rather than themselves. This is the *bureaucracy cop-out*. Therefore, it's not surprising that I consider this kind of ritualistic dissatisfaction harmless and a predictable part of any hierarchy. Unless it characterizes a disproportionate number of executives, it shouldn't be taken seriously, for to do so *also* ignores the human factor—this time, a negative side of it.

The Pecking Order

Some years ago, I came across material germane to this point. It comes from ethologist Konrad Lorenz, and is contained in his book, *On Aggression*. In the Berlin Zoo, Lorenz ". . . watched two strong, old male baboons assaulting each other in earnest for a minute. A moment later, one of them fled, hotly pursued by the other, who finally chased him into a corner. Unable to escape, the loser ran after him and presented his colorful hindquarters so persistently that the stronger one eventually 'acknowledged' his submissiveness by mounting him with a bored expression and performing a few perfunctory copulatory movements. Only then was the submissive one apparently satisfied that his rebellion had been forgiven."

Lorenz concludes that order (i.e., knowing one's place in the pecking order) is more important than self-assertion. In the structured society, the demand for order and to know one's place in it seems to be the most common denominator of animal and human behavior. We all know that in the corporation a similar demand operates. At the expense of efficiency and self-assertion, many executives will sacrifice all other corporate concerns to keeping their place, despite their complaints that keeping their place is what they dislike.

The Ritual Gripers

It's not overreaching to say that among the ritual gripers, their discontent with so-called bureaucracy is personal immaturity. When one listens carefully to an executive complain that his company is unresponsive to new ideas, it usually develops that what he means is that his boss is unresponsive to *his* ideas. Admittedly, many good ideas are spurned by dull-witted or insecure bosses. But it seems that more often ideas are spurned because subordinates haven't done their homework, or have used poor judgment in making recommendations. And it is the subordinate who uses poor judgment, or hasn't done his homework, who sulks the most when he learns that he hasn't come up with a suitable idea.

A subordinate may pout because he thinks his initiative has been rejected, and that he is justified in griping about the "bureaucracy" in his company. Another view, however, is that in all likelihood, his lackluster performance is anything but self-assertion, and is a face-saving, riskless way of saying, "I tried."

II

Bureaucracy's Failures;
People's Evasions

It should be clear that it is not to the common complaints of bureaucracy that we must turn to see the most harmful effects typical of the bureaucratic system. There is something else. Summing up, that "something else" turns out to be two-fold. There are two roles most bureaucracies perform poorly: (1) to discover and nurture extraordinary talent, and (2) to convey untainted information to top management. In times of stress, these shortcomings are fatal. In fact, when bureaucratic boondoggling becomes fatal, these faults often are so intertwined that it is impossible to find one without the other.

The first dysfunction flies in the face of the maxim that you can't keep a good person down. But as is painfully apparent, talented people often are driven out of corporations because their superiors fear them or are too dull to recognize their value. If the nurturing of talent isn't meticulously undertaken, corporations will stifle imagination and lose their best people. As they lose their best people, they lose their adaptability to new developments that either promise renewed vigor or threaten the company with obsolescence. Enough said, I think.

Tainted Information
The second dysfunction of bureaucracy is not so well understood. It involves the distortion of information prepared for top management. Such information gets tailored to serve the interests of the reporting department rather than the whole corporation. Sometimes this bending of the truth is intentional, as when costs are hidden to make an operation look

more profitable than it is. Sometimes it is unintentional, as when a sales manager uses his influence to divert money from R&D to his own division without realizing that the product he markets is noncompetitive, and without new developments, no sales force in the world can sell it. Then, for example, when the scientists in R&D are loathe to talk with sales over their slight, and neither talks with market research, a balanced presentation is impossible.

A story I told in *Confessions of a Corporate Headhunter* bears retelling here. It illustrates my point about tainted information and offers a lesson on dehumanization as well. It concerns an executive who was the director of internal consulting at a large corporation. The operations of this company were highly compartmentalized. Not only were scores of technical projects going on at the same time, but the firm's various financial service groups were vying with each other to gain financial control responsibilities over its many divisions. It was difficult for the managers of one operation to stay in touch with the managers of another. Yet coordination was a necessity. If top management was to be wise in allocating funds for the fiscal year, it had to grasp the goals of each division's projects, the costs to carry them out, and how long before they generated profit. This is where the internal consultant came in.

The Parochial Advocate

It is natural that each division manager make the strongest case for his division's projects. In fact, he is supposed to be prejudiced about what he parochially judges to be the interests of his division. Most division managers proceed on the basis that the company-wide point of view is the responsibility of top management.

Theoretically, parochial advocacy presupposes that each manager will make the strongest case possible for his project when he has his day in court. When all the divisional pitches are made, the chief executive officer then will choose from the alternatives. This sounds good, but in practice there are two obstacles to the ideal operation of this method.

First, the parochial advocate, by definition of his role, cannot be objective. For example, the technical problems his division faces in developing a new product get dressed up as "temporary design flaws soon to be conquered." The high cost of new machine tools is glossed over by a persuasive discussion of the savings the new machinery will afford. The cost of training a new sales force is played down in favor of the volume the new sales force (of course) will generate. The effect of these minor distortions is that top management bases its decisions on doctored data. And once a division manager gets his way by strengthening his case this way, his success spurs his peers to compete with him in distorting the evidence.

The other built-in danger of the bureaucratic, parochial advocate's method resides with top management. Ideally, each manager should be thought of as an equal among his competing managers. The basis on which top management should judge his case is the evidence in his presentation. In fact, however, certain managers stockpile influence just because their previous projects were favored by top management. The process snowballs. Because a certain manager got his way to build a new auto battery in his division, and because that operation was successful, that manager's fiscal year looks splendid and his requests for new funds acquire a bogus glitter. His new requests for funds have more influence than if they were compared only with the merits of competing requests.

To make parochial advocacy work, top management needs a trustworthy report of the operations of its divisions. This information won't come from a source identified with any single operation. What is needed is an unbiased overview stemming from a working knowledge of each division. Such a source of information (whether a person or group) has to move comfortably between the headquarters and the divisions, without appearing to be a corporate fink on the one hand, or a special pleader for line management on the other.

The internal consultant was just such a source of information. He joined the firm straight out of college, and early in his career was exposed to the most basic tasks. In the next twenty-five years he worked in virtually all of the company's divisions and rose steadily to his present delicate position. Because I knew this man well, it came as a disappointment to me when his career advancement came to an abrupt halt and he was let go. Moreover, adding insult to injury, a much younger executive was assigned to this job he had done so loyally and well and was made a vice-president!

Early Reward and Late Punishment

The intertwined lesson on bureaucratic dehumanization in this case is sad. Because this executive made himself indispensable in a certain function, top management had long hesitated to move him elsewhere. But now, if the option to move back to a divisional manager's job were offered to him, he felt he couldn't take it because such a move would *look* like a demotion. Not only that, he had lost the parochiality necessary to plead divisional interests fervently. Of course, it was this man's very removal from advocacy that made him vital. Now his objectivity and subservience to top management had rendered him not enough his own man for the virile policy cadres at the top.

The upshot of this irony is that bureaucracy attacked virtue in its two deadly ways: First, because top management knew that reports from its divisional managers would be less than truth, it needed someone to mediate between fact and fiction. Second, because the image of *hierarchical promotion* had become stamped within the corporate mind, the executive who served the firm's highest needs found himself outside the pecking order where he lacked the clout enjoyed by his bureaucratic peers. Extraordinary talent had gone unnurtured.

The main organizational issue in this case is not that this man lost his vitality (demonstrated when he, but not his function, was eliminated), but that bureaucracy earlier rewarded him for conforming to its needs, then later punished him *because* he had. Except for those resting at the pinnacle of talent or wariness, most people don't bridge such gaps. Consequently, corporations need to look beyond the Peter Principle, since it is clear that people *drift* as well as rise to the level of their incompetence.

The Individual Issue

Now let's shift gears a bit. A moment ago, I said the *organizational* issue surrounding the internal consultant is not that this man had lost his vitality, but that bureaucracy rewarded him initially for conforming to its needs, then later punished him because he had.

In discussing bureaucracy, it is important to distinguish between the organizational and the *individual* issues. While most of the points that I've made so far in this appendix have to do with organizational matters, I would like to return to a theme touched on earlier to make this distinction. In doing so, let me reemphasize that while bureaucracy can and does victimize individuals, many so-called bureaucratic injustices are actually "victim-precipitated." That is, the individual has not exercised the control over his work situation that he truly has at his disposal. That is the individual issue, and is the other side of this two-way street called bureaucracy.

In considering the individual issue, think about yourself. For the time being, suspend your thoughts on how bureaucracy affects your job, and concentrate on how you impact the bureaucracy in and around that job. If you are like most of us, it is easy to forget that as a member of management, *you are bureaucracy!*

How easy it is to take refuge in bureaucracy when it suits our designs but to flee it when it frustrates our purposes. How easy it is to believe in the orderliness of bureaucracy when we're not in a hurry but to decry its cumbersomeness when we're impatient. How easy it is to believe we practice the science of management with our subordinates but are browbeaten by our superiors.

The Round Robin of Low Expectations

An example of victim-precipitated bureaucracy is the syndrome in which we make the boss, instead of ourselves, the fall guy. It is a round robin of low expectations. We all trap ourselves this way to some extent. Here's how this five-step, self-debilitating process works:

First, the executive is presented with a task where he wants to shine, but where, for some reason, he questions his ability to perform well. The boss calls him in and says, "Joe, I want you to design a new inventory control system."

Second, after taking on the assignment, Joe unwittingly adopts a self-fulfilling prophecy. He says something like, "The boss won't like it," or, "Nobody's gonna help me on this baby."

Third, he turns in a riskless, lackluster performance that actually assures rejection of the proposal. The gut feel beneath this is: "My God, if I do my *best* and my boss rejects it, I couldn't stand it!"

Fourth, Joe engages in face-saving blame. He says to himself, "If the boss weren't so closed-minded, I could design a system that works beautifully!"

Fifth, by participating in this underground process, Joe lowers his self-esteem for facing other tasks. He avoids them while trying to act *as if* he's making a contribution.

The round robin of low expectations is the strange way Joe grooms himself for failure. It is a self-set trap. He fools himself with it because subjectively, he feels excused. But, objectively, he fails. And as enough of us fail, so do our companies. The Joes and the devalued internal consultant in my earlier example may well start out their careers with enthusiasm and their skills well burnished. But somewhere along the line, they allow their vitality to be sapped—mainly by *letting* bureaucracy "do its number" on them. Bureaucracy must be served to provide order for the corporation, but it must be *challenged*, too. The achiever conforms to a point, but constructively tests bureaucracy's borders and limits routinely. What many of us forget is that bureaucracy itself evolves—must evolve—in order to serve its purpose in its constantly evolving environment. It evolves by solid, imaginative, judicious achievers not creating upheaval and revolution, but by keeping tension on bureaucracy's leash. Ironically, bureaucracy rewards such behavior.

III

Organizational and Mental Health

It is apparent that resolving the antagonism that exists between the individual and the organization is always difficult. In fact, the modern corporation is so complex that such a resolution never can be total. Yet I think we're moving in the right direction.

So do others. For example, Warren Bennis, in his incisive book, *Beyond Bureaucracy,* makes this observation: "There is an interesting historical parallel between the development of criteria for the evaluation of mental health and evolution of standards for evaluating organizational health." He goes on to say that the main reason for the coming together of the theories of organizational and mental health is quite simple. The methods of a more scientific management and psychotherapy have the same goal: to perceive reality, both internal and external, and to face those realities in order to act intelligently.

By recognizing that the goals of organizational and mental health are the same, Bennis provides the perspective necessary to look down the road toward the blending of corporate and individual needs. And this perspective encourages the corporation to explore ways to spur men and women to act on the unique strengths they truly possess, but of which they may not be aware.

The Corporate Life Cycle and Individual Strengths
If we cast an analytical eye at the life of any corporation, it can be said to pass through four stages:

○ *Birth and Creativity:* when the company struggles for survival, is characterized by unusual camaraderie, and is run by a charismatic leader.

○ *Power and Growth:* when systems and procedures replace informality and randomness; administrators replace entrepreneurs, and dignity replaces spontaneity.

○ *Obsolescence and Decay:* when in failing to adapt to evolutionary change, corporate leaders are suspect for their motives, criticized for laxity in responding to opportunity, and search for cosmetic ways to repair their damaged image.

○ *Death or Rebirth:* when a company either adapts to change or dies.

The IBMs, 3Ms, P&Gs and GEs, etc., that I mentioned in my opening remarks to Section I are examples of superior companies prolonging the power and growth stage by adapting to evolutionary change. As I said there, their permanence is proof of adaptability. On the other hand, for rebirth to take place in a company, its leaders must be willing to undergo enormous revisions of structures, attitudes, and objectives. Since top management usually has grown comfortable with the status quo, typically they, along with the chief executive, are replaced by new executives.

To be sure, there are exceptions. For some years, I have observed firsthand and admired the top management of a company that is one of America's largest industrial corporations; one that in the late sixties faced the choice of death or rebirth. The chairman and president, both long-termers with the firm, courageously took the actions necessary to reshape the entire makeup and philosophy of the firm—setting it on a course for rebirth. Today it stands as a model company that has been featured in most major business magazines. Such cases are rare.

The corporation committed to averting death by adapting to evolutionary change is well advised to return to Peter Drucker's observation that effective executives are those who have *learned* how to make their strengths productive. It is only when its executives become such achievers that a corporation excels.

However, Drucker's observation implies a hidden problem that first must be recognized. That is, as I pointed out in chapter 3, executives often think they know what their strengths are, but really don't, even when they are quite accomplished. They have been socialized to want and cultivate certain strengths without stopping to notice what their real strengths are. Boiled down, what this means is that scores of executives attempt self-*image* actualization on the job instead of self-actualization. This is not rewarding for self, and in the long run, is not productive for the company.

Averting Corporate Death by Tapping Buried Strengths

What is required of the corporation is that it stop thinking of an executive's strengths solely in terms of his or her credentials or bureaucratic role. That's dehumanizing, and in the last analysis, is how corporations die. Increasingly, we have to elicit and accommodate the executive's distinctive strengths that go beyond any current or future job description.

In short, for a company to remain adaptable, it has to open the way for its executives to be achievers. To do that, the company has to realize that it is in the business of helping its executives *learn* what their unique strengths are and how to make those strengths productive.

Let me cite a concrete example of how I have seen this work: On occasion I conduct what I call "action perspectives workshops" for top executives, each participant coming from a different company. For four days, eight able executives and I salt ourselves away at a remote resort in what is, for these people, a courageous experiment. It is courageous because they have never attempted anything like this before.

While I call these small group meetings "action perspectives workshops," I think of them as "wake-up sessions" for achievers. They are workshops to *wake up* executives to

strengths, abilities, desires, creativity, values, likes, and dis-
likes they not only aren't expressing, but aren't even aware
they possess. I use mainly role-playing techniques to help
these executives reclaim such disowned strengths and become the achievers they are meant to be.

In one of these workshops, I couldn't help noticing an
executive in attendance who was the vice-president of manufacturing of one of our major food producing companies.
He was a terribly nice person, but it seemed to me he was
too nice, *too* ingratiating, *too* accommodating. The workshop
got fascinating when I asked him to take on the role of an
independent cat, the kind who always looks the other way
when his master walks into the room and seeks his attention.

As a foil to this cat-playing executive, the other members
of the group were told that they each in turn would play a
frolicking, affectionate puppy who would for a few minutes
carry on a conversation with this cat. This activity required,
then, that the cat-player hold his own against the other seven
puppy-players. Neither he nor his antagonists were given any
instructions on what to say to each other. The successive
scenes rolled out as the players devised their "scripts" on
the spot.

What occurred was an unforgettable lesson on human
development. All the players lost their self-consciousness and
got engrossed in their roles. The cat-playing executive increasingly took charge of the exchanges and began to show
his contempt for what he termed "the sycophantic, slobber-
ing puppy who has no mind of his own, nor any backbone."

The lesson is obvious and need not be dealt with at
length. Suffice it to say that the cat-playing executive made
clear to himself that he could be far more true to his nature
by being decisive, holding firm opinions, and expressing them
without fear of rejection than he could be with his typical,
all-too-submissive actions. He admitted to the group that he
worked much too hard at being a nice guy and that his boss
had dropped hints that he should take firmer stands—even

with him!—and quit worrying about the repercussions. He also said he found the exercise exhilarating and couldn't wait to get back to his job.

I'm not current on how this executive is faring today. But over a year after the session, he told me the experience had a great impact on his self-perception and output. Given that he already was successful in a key spot with a top company, it's hard to say what that's worth to him and his firm.

This executive's experience was repeated with the other members of the group who were assigned roles appropriate to them. Similar results were achieved. Such exercises reveal what can happen if the corporation is bent on devising ways to elicit the distinctive, neglected resources of its executives rather than their formalized, commonplace performance. Two crucial needs can be met at the same time: (1) the corporation gets the imagination and talent it needs, thus maintaining its organizational health; and (2) the individual gets the emotional rewards from giving what he's got beyond bureaucracy's definition of his job, thus maintaining his mental health. The dehumanizing elements of bureaucracy are softened, and the corporation's chances for distinctive achievement are enhanced.

IV

How to Make Use of Task Forces

I concluded the previous chapter by citing the example of an executive who learned how he could become more of an achiever and contributor to his corporation by reclaiming his disowned strengths. I concluded the chapter before that by saying achievers are those who judiciously give expression to their unique strengths, and in so doing, *aid* their companies by stretching bureaucracy's limits. Earlier, in chapter 10, I said that the achiever approaches his or her work with a task-force mentality. Then in chapter 19, I argued that for an executive to be an achiever, he or she must be a facilitator.

This chapter is intended to show how (1) corporations can encourage the achiever to give expression to unique strengths; (2) facilitative skills can be used in a rationally designed way; and (3) the corporation can benefit from having bureaucracy modified, or in some cases, circumvented, by making use of task forces.

Students of organization attuned to good human relations, but leery of panaceas, have returned to the conviction that there is no ideal design for organizational structure. While authoritarianism is a bygone mode, due primarily to the independence and professionalism of the technocrats, the corporate pyramid is still with us. And rightly so. No one has found a suitable substitute for it. It remains the best way to organize people and tasks on a large scale.

However, for almost any company, an important structural requirement is flexibility. For a company to innovate, to meet new market opportunities, it must be willing to adapt to change. So as long as the pyramid is with us, a looser hierarchy with open and full communication is essential for companies facing new challenges and opportunities.

One way a corporation can meet new challenges and opportunities is through task forces. Task forces are interdisciplinary *ad hoc* groups assembled within the company to solve problems. They are relatively short-lived, disbanded upon reaching their goals.

Task forces have become necessary because the typical pyramidal hierarchy of the corporation with its man-in-box, departmentalized outlook—while well-equipped to handle daily operations—is not adaptable and quick enough to deal effectively with unanticipated challenges that are often interdepartmental or interdisciplinary in nature. Accordingly, the hierarchy often cannot meet such unanticipated problems with relish or clarity of purpose.

As I indicated in chapter 9, line and staff have become fuzzy designations. In addition, the lines between the disciplines (e.g., finance and marketing), though drawn as arbitrarily as ever, become increasingly artificial. Today, companies are pluralistic. Their organizational problems are similar to the social problems of society at large. The larger the company, the more complex the web of interacting vested interest groups with varying traditions, objectives, values, and beliefs.

Task forces, far from being a panacea, have many pitfalls. But with their flexibility and overlapping quality, they offer a great deal for gaining cooperation between intracorporate fiefdoms. Nor are they very new. Companies have always turned to key groups to deal with special projects. But very few have set up an ongoing programmatic task-force management system to deal with new challenges and unanticipated problems, and to be managed as a factory or market research department is managed. For example, I have yet to hear of a company that has a position entitled *Vice-President of Task-Force Management.* I'm suggesting that many companies should establish such a position.

Operating Challenges of Task Forces

Before a corporation can make a task-force system work, it needs to have a good idea of how task forces themselves operate. They are a good deal more complex than meets the eye. Yet for the managements willing to spend time and effort experimenting with task forces until they "get it right," great benefits accrue, not the least of which is giving room to achievers to bring their formidable talents to bear on corporate causes.

The way to start in making a task-force system work is, first of all, to realize that each task force is distinguished by its size, makeup, and purpose. Second, all task forces face similar operating problems surrounding: (1) objectives, (2) membership, (3) roles, (4) values, (5) procedures, (6) communication, (7) direction, and (8) decision making. A summary of these operating problems follows.

Objectives It is imperative that a task force know what it is out to accomplish. This is achieved through setting clear objectives and refining them as conditions change. If a task force does not have clear objectives, then more time will be required to fulfill its purpose. If it takes the additional time up front to set clear objectives, less time will be required to achieve them. The common problem, however, is that objectives are not understood or believed in by all the members of the task force. It is easy to think that the objective of a task force is simply to solve the problem it has been assigned to solve.

For example, a marketing vice-president of a national retail chain might assign a task force to formulate a uniform pricing system. Let us assume he does so because he is inundated by complaints from the field involving conflicts between merchandise managers, store managers, and district managers over pricing of merchandise. After analyzing the "pricing problem," the task force working with clarity may discover it is a symptom of a less obvious, more general problem that involves all of top management, not merely the marketing department. They may discover that the conflicts between the various managers are not caused by disagreements over pricing as such, but because there is no final authority for making *all* merchandising decisions, one of which is pricing. The problem becomes one of communication instead of pricing, and may also include purchasing and distribution considerations.

Whether the corporation concludes that one person will make final merchandising decisions or that they should be made in interdepartmental committee, it can structure its lines of communication accordingly. The task force will have done its job; top management can act on what has been uncovered.

Membership Criteria Who belongs? Who should be included? These are important questions in assembling a task force. The explicit criteria for membership surround the broad definition of the business problem, but the breadth of membership is important for two reasons: (1) diverse skills and interests can be applied to problems which turn out to be not what were expected; and (2) task forces with overly homogeneous membership become inert and unimaginative. It is true that too much dissimilarity makes agreement impossible, but too little leads to a task force without spark.

Clarification of Roles Clarity of roles, including leadership roles, is essential if a task force is to function properly. Influential as well as official leaders should be identified. Each member should understand his role and have it made clear to all the others.

It is obvious that confusion reigns when roles are confused. But it is not so well known that task forces are more effective when members' roles are clear to each other and understood in terms of intracompany influence and prestige. It would be ideal if all members displayed an equal sense of obligation, but experience and small-group research confirm that this simply does not occur.

Shared Values Task-force members must share similar values. Popular press about "sensitivity training" to the contrary, it seems more likely that successful task forces are made up of members who already share similar values, rather than those who have their values reshaped by each other. Discernment of shared values becomes important in selecting members who will work together on a task force.

Defined Procedures Procedures already are shaped a good deal by where the task force stands on its objectives and the criteria of its membership, clarification of their roles, and the values that they share. In turn, procedures shape the actual means of task-force communication, direction, and decision making.

At the outset, or during the course of group functioning when procedures may be revised or refined, they need to be defined, accepted, and followed on the whole by the members for the task force to maintain orderliness.

Unfiltered Communication Successful task-force communication is free and crisscross; everybody talks with everybody else. Though it risks trivia, each member is encouraged to share his or her ideas and feelings whenever they are considered relevant to problem solving. Sometimes personal data is shared. Sometimes it is criticized. Other times it isn't. In either case, it is reacted to openly within the group. In the successful task force, no one holds back information for reasons of fear, ridicule, or rejection. Nor does any member withhold his or her contribution while the task force is struggling at length with a knotty problem.

A Sense of Direction It is common for task forces to lose their sense of direction. Since stated business problems often end up being not the real problems, a task force may have to revise its objectives. Seeing a need for change in objectives sometimes is difficult because a task force can get mired in detailed analysis and lose perspective. In addition, membership problems can arise from revised objectives. One or more members may not believe in the revised goals. Or they may believe in them only up to a point and may want to disengage from the group when that point is reached.

If some members leave the task force, decisions have to be made about replacing them with people who share belief in the revised objectives. When there is succession of membership, the task force changes. The changes may or may not be beneficial to group functioning. It is the responsibility of the task-force leader or facilitator to keep the task force from going astray. Any time the facilitator asks the task force to pause and see if it is still on the right track, he risks consideration of new objectives and the consequent loss of a member or two.

The facilitator has to be prepared to take this risk and work at maintaining cohesion. He also has to be prepared for periods of unpopularity when he interrupts task-force movement by asking the members to consider if they are moving in the right direction, or pushing them to reach decisions when there is a deadline to meet.

Collaborated Decision Making Ideally, task-force decisions are collaborative decisions. Everyone participates. Everyone is given a voice. Majority vote and minority bulldozing are avoided. Decisions are faced up to and made when the task force reaches a point at which they should be made; when purposeful action is indicated; when all alternatives and their consequences have been analyzed as carefully as possible, and the one best choice from among many options must be recommended to the ultimate decision maker.

Admittedly, task forces will many times fall short of ideal decision making. Immediate priorities and deadlines often will force a majority vote, a powerful minority's bull-dozing, or the leader's arbitrary choice. But the frequency of these shortcomings will be reduced in companies that expect task-force members somehow to come to *agreement* among themselves.

Of course, a task-force *system* by itself is not the main way for corporations to direct their people to autonomous, spontaneous, quality performance. But it is *one* way to do so, and can be far more encompassing in scope throughout a company than many managements imagine. What remains is for a company to enlist the best efforts possible from all of its people by ensuring that the "we" feeling, the feeling of belonging, is tucked into every nook and cranny of its operations. The absolute necessity for our corporations to do this is the subject of the next, concluding chapter of this appendix.

V

Interpersonal Competence: The Last Two Words on Corporate Achievement

It's obvious to the point of embarrassment to observe that among corporations one of the major differences between winners and losers is how their people are handled. Winning companies are good people handlers. Losers are not. Yawn!

Yet what is more difficult than prescribing methods that ensure competent people handling? And what is good people handling anyway? Isn't it different for everybody?

Such questions concerning the large intangibles that face all of us directly—both as they relate to us personally and in the way we manage our subordinates—continue to gnaw at us. They are so big and amorphous there seems no way to address them meaningfully. Certainly, enhancing the way the entire work force of a company is handled is one of those gigantic intangibles that form the very essence of effective management of the enterprises of which we are a part. But how do we pull if off?

Hard as we've tried, we executive development specialists haven't provided the answers on this subject. However, what we have provided are concepts and language helpful to our thinking more clearly about this business of better people handling.

Corporations Are People
To my mind, the most important people-handling concept is that of *interpersonal competence*. It underscores the fact that in the last analysis a corporation is nothing but an inter-

dependent collection of people organized around a mission (no matter how loosely defined or understood). In other words, it is an interpersonal network. Those companies that have a reputation for handling their people well have mastered interpersonal competence. Rightly so, they are the envy of most of us.

The most authoritative analysis of interpersonal competence has been offered by Chris Argyris of the Harvard Business School. In his book, *Interpersonal Competence and Organizational Effectiveness,* he defines interpersonal competence as "the individual's ability to produce intended effects in such a way that he can continue to do so." His definition is a good one because it takes into account the rational and emotional elements of a company. It recognizes the rational objectives of the structural organization that have to be met to some degree if the company is to remain viable. But it also includes the emotional needs of the human organization that have to be met to gain cooperation in reaching these rational objectives.

Problems of any company are not truly solved if the methods used alienate and demean people. In such cases, the solutions are only temporary, and the methods cannot be used again to solve other problems. People close ranks and those offended employ evasive tactics to make sure they aren't abused in the future. Knowing that the successful performance of our corporations is dependent on us, what all achievers in management need to learn is how to produce intended effects in such a way that we can continue to do so.

Benefits to be Gained
What follows is not a grand prescription to master the specifics of company-wide interpersonal competence. But it is an attempt to offer some general discussion on interpersonal competence, and what I see as the six broad benefits to any company that wants to work at putting interpersonal competence into practice.

Mutual Trust and Understanding A company that invites suspicion from its people invites trouble. Conversely, the company that conveys an attitude from its senior management that its people are valued friends is well on its way to winning their unqualified support. The "we" feeling permeates the atmosphere of the company and provides everyone with a central company consciousness—pride at sharing in the corporate identity.

Trust conveys belief in one's ability to render independent judgments and carry out independent action without harm to the one extending the privilege of such independence. Understanding conveys an acceptance of rationale of one's actions whether that rationale is agreed with or not. Corporations can't allow such liberties to be abused to the extent that their moorings become wobbly, but they can attempt to make them available to as many people as possible. This is what is behind the growth in "quality circles" abroad, and increasingly in this country.

Increased Self-Confidence and Esteem It seems axiomatic that a person believes in himself to the extent that those around him whom he respects indicate they believe in him. This is not to say that one loses all sense of selfhood if he finds himself in hostile territory where his ideas or character come under attack. But it does say that withstanding such attacks assumes a stored-up sense of worth acquired at an earlier time.

It also is true that no matter how firmly embedded, such self-confidence and deeply ingrained convictions can be whittled away under a controlled, systematic onslaught. The experience of our servicemen taken prisoner during the Korean War and subjected to Communist brainwashing with distressing results is proof of this. As is Patricia Hearst. As is Jonestown.

Therefore, we can assume that those companies that devise programs to increase their people's feeling of self-confidence and esteem are precisely those that will have lower turnover and more loyalty.

Self-confidence and esteem don't come from gold watches for longevity, trips to Hawaii for sales contest winners, or raises in pay in automatic increments. As important as those things are in specific circumstances, they are worthless unless they occur within a corporate-wide context that generates inarticulate comments such as "My company treats people like people." This is unimpressive language to be sure, but it indicates an *attitude* that makes rubbish of the lofty rhetoric about "human ideals" in companies where similar attitudes don't exist.

One large firm that has impressed me by generating self-esteem more than many others of comparable complexity is Caterpillar Tractor Company. In two decades as an executive recruiter, I have had at least some contact with middle- and top-management executives in most major companies in the United States. In my view, few can match the self-esteem Caterpillar nurtures in its people. And I say this depite the company's having undergone an eight-month strike in 1982–83. I should say that Caterpillar isn't my client. I reached this conclusion because of my failure to recruit executives away from them to a client who is a competitor in the earth-moving business!

Any large company, Caterpillar included, depends on the actions of large numbers of people who are marked by average abilities. The key to meeting corporate objectives is to get these average people to pull together in performing a myriad of interrelated functions. If Thoreau was right when he said that the mass of men lead lives of quiet desperation, this is less so in the case of companies like Caterpillar where almost 100,000 people benefit from a senior management committed to interpersonal competence.

Lowered Dependence and Increased Risk Taking for Decision Makers A decentralized management organization should be the ideal of every company serious about increasing its interpersonal competence. In theory, decentralization is an attempt to submerge decision making and responsibility to the lowest point possible in the corporation. The word *lowest* is used because decentralization takes place in the pyramid of organizational structure. The president sits on top while endless gradations of subordinates fan out underneath.

Decentralization has not lived up to its promise, with the result that many companies have gone back to a more centralized form of management. The most frequent complaint I have heard from top executives about decentralization is that there are few managers who can "hack it" with the pressures that accompany autonomy, profit responsibility, and decision making.

While it is true that some top executives are copping out with such complaints and concealing their reluctance to give up prerogatives, it is not so with all of them. The lament of many is legitimate. They can't find enough achievers eager and able to assume such burdens. Of course, the "right" executives thrive on such responsibilities. They don't consider them burdens, but opportunities.

It is the rare individual who jumps into the saddle with the fervor of a (Teddy) Roosevelt Rough Rider. It is a commentary on our level of interpersonal competence that we cannot recognize younger persons coming along within our companies who possess such qualities. These are the achievers who need development mainly and simply through proper on-the-job exposures more than through formal "management development" programs.

Top management should make every attempt to scout their entire company thoroughly to uncover the kinds of managers who will thrive in the decentralized mode. With its ever-increasing competitive pressures, modern business seems not to generate the very spirit it needs more than any other: entrepreneurialism. Decentralization fosters entrepreneurial thinking by forcing on its achievers lowered dependency and increased risk taking. And lowered dependence and risk taking are examples of interpersonal competence in action.

Lowered Conformity and Increased Innovation Excessive conformity is stifling. It robs any human situation of its creative flow—of innovation. Innovation's child, at least in a corporate marketing sense, is a new product or service. Without new products or services, a company stagnates and dies. We live in a time when the need for new products and services is greater than ever for the sake of corporate survival, but also when the life cycle of any product or service becomes shorter because of the stepped-up pace of our existence. Accordingly, a company with a management predeliction for enforcing outmoded ways of thinking and acting, based on an authoritarian style and centralized chain of command, will find its nostrils assaulted as it cleans up after the circus parade.

Speaking of rear-action movements, I would like to recount a striking example of how an _open, experimental atmosphere_ existing in a company can result in unique solutions to persistent problems. It is described in William Gordon's book, _Synectics._

A technical group was faced with the problem of inventing a dispenser which could be used with liquid products as varied as glue and nail polish. It was necessary that the dispenser be one piece without a top to be removed and replaced with each use. The specifications required that the dispenser's mouth be designed to open for dispensing and close tightly after each use. Group members directed themselves to a _new way of thinking_ about the problem. They asked themselves what actions in nature operated the way the dispenser must. The following discussion ensued:

A: "A clam sticks its neck out of its shell . . . brings the neck back in and closes the shell again."

B: "Yeah, but the clam's shell is an exoskeleton. The real part, the real anatomy of the clam is inside."

C: "What difference does that make?"

A: "Well, the neck of the clam doesn't clean itself . . . it just drags itself back into the protection of the shell."

D: "What other analogies are there to the problem?"

E: "How about the human mouth?"

B: "What does it dispense?"

E: "Spit . . . the mouth propels spit out whenever it wants . . . oh, oh. It isn't really self-cleaning . . . you know, dribbling on the chin."

A: "Couldn't there be a mouth which was trained so that it wouldn't dribble?"

E: "Maybe, but it would be contrived as hell . . . and if the human mouth can't keep itself clean with all the feedback in the human system . . ."

D: "When I was a kid I grew up on a farm. I used to drive a hayrack behind a pair of draft horses. When a horse would take a crap, first his outer . . . I guess you'd call it a kind of mouth, would open. Then the anal sphincter would dilate and a horse ball would come out. Afterwards, everything would close up again. The whole picture would be clean as a whistle."

E: "What if the horse had diarrhea?"

D: "That happened when they got too much grain . . . but the horse would kind of wink a couple of times while the anal mouth was drawn back . . . the winking would squeeze out the liquid . . . then the outer mouth would cover the whole thing up again."

E: "You're describing a plastic motion."

D: "I guess so . . . could we simulate the horse's ass in plastic?"

These fellows did. The *eureka* occurs with more regularity in companies that work on interpersonal competence.

Self-Fulfillment and Internal Commitment Self-fulfillment (or actualization if you prefer) comes to the achiever who has found his or her niche. There is no more rewarding experience for a person than to know he or she is playing on a team that values his or her contribution. I emphasize *team* because the analogy from sports—where a group of individuals become welded together in pursuit of a common goal—helps us visualize how a well-managed company gets all-out performance from its people.

Internal commitment blossoms when a person believes that the achievement of corporate objectives is partially dependent on him, and he wants to do all he can to see that they are met. He and company become inseparable in his mind, and his responsibilities—detailed in a job description tucked away somewhere in a personnel file drawer—is dry stuff compared to what he gives daily to the corporation. The rhetorical, external identity and demands of the company are brought inside the person where the seeds of commitment find fertile soil.

Self-fulfillment and internal commitment are each other's shadow. Both are cast in companies that are committed to their human resources.

Aspiration to Mastery Every person needs to master something. Executives, for example, choose careers in business with the thought that, all things considered, corporate life offers the greatest opportunity for vocational satisfaction. They come to the corporation of their own volition, and are resources that shouldn't be wasted.

Integral to a conception of job enrichment is an executive's awareness that he's good at something, that those around him realize it, and they, in turn, demonstrate in some way their admiration of his skill. In an open, receptive corporate atmosphere, an executive with any sense of himself and what he is about gladly gives his best efforts.

If a company is going to tap these rich resources, to set free these noble impulses residing in everyone, it has to reward achievement. And it should be remembered that the most important rewards to people are not financial, but emotional! Caterpillar, mentioned earlier, is not a high-paying company. The senior management of that company has found a way to filter *achievement recognition* throughout its ranks on a large scale. They have found a way to make most people earn respect in the eyes of their associates.

Limited Tasks and Objectives

Every corporation is based on a division of labor. This means that each individual and group responsible for doing something operates with limited tasks and objectives: tasks and objectives that fit into some sort of corporate whole. There are two good reasons for this basis of organization: (1) it takes advantage of specialized skills; and (2) it keeps any one person or group from wreaking havoc to monstrous proportions.

The disadvantage of this basis of organization is that the individual (even the CEO) sometimes longs for the satisfaction of the cobbler who made the whole shoe. Unlike the craftsman, he becomes frustrated and bored, puts a cap on his imagination, and seeks other trappings to substitute for the joys of a job well done.

In complex society, there's no way we can return to the cobbler's bench. But if we make the right moves, we certainly don't have to relinquish the joys of a job well done. What we have to do is provide our work forces with a climate where they feel encouraged to make contributions that are *uniquely theirs*.

This is not as difficult as it sounds, and it puts excitement back into the job. My purpose in this final chapter has been to remind us of what we already know—but may have forgotten—on how we can help bring this about.

B

CORRECT
ANSWERS
TO QUIZZES

Chapter 1   **Being Warm**
1. U/O   2. U/O   3. S/S   4. S/S   5.U/O
6. U/O   7. S/S   8. U/O   9. U/O   10. S/S

Chapter 2   **Practicing Listening**
1. S/S   2. S/S   3. U/O   4. U/O   5. S/S
6. U/O   7. U/O   8. U/O   9. U/O   10. S/S

Chapter 3   **Practicing Encouragement**
1. U/O   2. S/S   3. U/O   4. S/S   5. U/O
6. U/O   7. U/O   8. U/O   9. S/S   10. U/O

Chapter 4   **Thinking Positively**
1. S/S   2. S/S   3. U/O   4. U/O   5. S/S
6. U/O   7. S/S   8. S/S   9. S/S   10. U/O

Chapter 5   **Sharing Self, Time and Information**
1. U/O   2. S/S   3. U/O   4. S/S   5. S/S
6. S/S   7. S/S   8. S/S   9. S/S   10. U/O

Chapter 6   **Being Vulnerable**
1. S/S   2. S/S   3. S/S   4. U/O   5. U/O
6. U/O   7. U/O   8. S/S   9. U/O   10. U/O

Chapter 7   **Speaking One's Mind**
1. U/O   2. U/O   3. U/O   4. S/S   5. S/S
6. S/S   7. U/O   8. S/S   9. S/S   10. U/O

Chapter 8   **Being Experimental**
1. U/O   2. U/O   3. U/O   4. S/S   5. S/S
6. U/O   7. U/O   8. S/S   9. U/O   10. U/O

Chapter 9   **Making Bold Decisions**
1. S/S   2. S/S   3. S/S   4. U/O   5. U/O
6. U/O   7. U/O   8. S/S   9. S/S   10. U/O

Chapter 10 **Acting On Your Unique Strengths**
1. S/S   2. U/O   3. U/O   4. U/O   5. U/O
6. U/O   7. S/S   8. U/O   9. S/S   10. S/S

Chapter 11 **Making Judicious Decisions**
1. U/O   2. S/S   3. S/S   4. U/O   5. U/O
6. S/S   7. U/O   8. S/S   9. U/O   10. U/O

Chapter 12 **Setting Priorities**
1. S/S   2. U/O   3. U/O   4. U/O   5. S/S
6. S/S   7. U/O   8. U/O   9. U/O   10. U/O

Chapter 13 **Being Tenacious**
1. U/O   2. U/O   3. S/S   4. S/S   5. U/O
6. S/S   7. S/S   8. S/S   9. U/O   10. S/S

Chapter 14 **Being of Good Humor**
1. U/O   2. S/S   3. U/O   4. S/S   5. S/S
6. U/O   7. U/O   8. S/S   9. S/S   10. U/O

Chapter 15 **Being Lucky**
1. S/S   2. U/O   3. S/S   4. S/S   5. S/S
6. S/S   7. U/O   8. U/O   9. U/O   10. U/O

Chapter 16 **Delivering The Goods**
1. U/O   2. U/O   3. S/S   4. S/S   5. U/O
6. U/O   7. U/O   8. S/S   9. S/S   10. U/O

Chapter 17 **Thinking Beyond the Obvious**
1. S/S   2. U/O   3. S/S   4. U/O   5. U/O
6. U/O   7. S/S   8. U/O   9. U/O   10. S/S

Chapter 18 **Refining One's Gifts**
1. S/S   2. U/O   3. S/S   4. U/O   5. U/O
6. S/S   7. S/S   8. S/S   9. U/O   10. U/O

Chapter 19 **Being a Facilitator**

1. U/O	2. S/S	3. S/S	4. U/O	5. U/O
6. U/O	7. S/S	8. S/S	9. U/O	10. U/O

Chapter 20 **Exercising Vision**

1. U/O	2. U/O	3. U/O	4. S/S	5. U/O
6. S/S	7. S/S	8. U/O	9. S/S	10. S/S

BIBLIOGRAPHY

Adler, Alfred. *The Science of Living.* Edited by Heinz L. Ansbacher. New York: Doubleday Anchor, 1969.
_____. *Social Interest: A Challenge to Mankind.* New York: Capricorn, 1964.

Argyris, Chris. *Interpersonal Competence and Organizational Effectiveness.* Homewood, Illinois: Richard D. Irwin, 1962.

Bach, Richard, *Illusions.* New York: Dell, 1979.

Bennis, Warren. *Beyond Bureaucracy.* New York: McGraw-Hill Paperback, 1973. (Original hardcover: *Changing Organizations.* New York: McGraw-Hill, 1966.)

Cousins, Norman. *Anatomy of an Illness.* New York: W.W. Norton, 1979.

Cox, Allan. *Confessions of a Corporate Headhunter.* New York: Trident, 1973.
_____. *The Cox Report on the American Corporation.* New York: Delacorte, 1982.

Drucker, Peter F. *The Effective Executive.* New York: Harper & Row, 1967.

Epictetus. *The Discourses of Epictetus.* Translated by George Long. Vol. 12, *Great Books of the Western World.* Chicago: Encyclopaedia Brittanica, 1952.

Gordon, Mary. *The Company of Women.* New York: Random House, 1980.

Gordon, William J. J. *Synectics.* New York: Harper & Row, 1961.

Hoffer, Eric. *Reflections on the Human Condition.* New York: Harper & Row, 1973.

Horney, Karen. *Our Inner Conflicts.* New York: W.W. Norton, 1945.

James, William. *The Principles of Psychology.* New York: Dover Publications, 1950.

Liebling, A. J. *Chicago, The Second City.* New York: Alfred A. Knopf, 1952.

Lorenz, Konrad. *On Aggression.* New York: Harcourt, Brace & World, 1966.

McLuhan, Marshall. *Culture Is Our Business.* New York: McGraw-Hill, 1970.

Melville, Herman. *Moby Dick.* New York: Dodd, Mead, 1923.

Moore, Wilbert. *The Conduct of the Corporation*. New York: Random House, 1962.

Naisbitt, John. *Megatrends*. New York: Warner, 1982.

Perls, Frederick. *Gestalt Therapy Verbatim*. Lafayette, California: Real People Press, 1969.

Peter, Laurence J. and Hill, Raymond. *The Peter Principle*. New York: William Morrow, 1969.

Toffler, Alvin. *Future Shock*. New York: Random House, 1970.

Van Dusen, Wilson. *The Natural Depth in Man*. New York: Harper & Row, 1972.

Weber, Max. *Max Weber*. Selections from his work edited by S. M. Miller. New York: Thomas Y. Crowell, 1963.

Index